THE LIFESTYLE OF WORSHIP
BY
LEAH LEWIS

The Lifestyle of WORSHIP

OUT OF THE WORLD & INTO THE KINGDOM

By:

LEAH LEWIS

Unless otherwise stated, all Scripture quotations are taken from the *New King James Version* of the Holy Bible. Copyright © 1979, 1980, 1982, 1984 by Thomas Nelson, Inc. Publishers. Used by permission. All rights reserved. Scripture quotations marked (KJV) are from the *King James Version* of the Holy Bible.

THE LIFESTYLE OF WORSHIP
OUT OF THE WORLD & INTO THE KINGDOM

Copyright © 2016 by Leah Lewis.
All rights reserved.
ISBN: 978-976-8260-64-2

Cover art by LillyWorks - Creative Design Services.
www.lillyworks.ml.

Published by Malkut Publishing.
www.malkut-publishing.com.

For information on bulk purchases and special pricing, or for any further information, please contact the publisher using any of the following means:
-Send an email to: info@malkut-publishing.com;
-Send postage to: POS10058, 4411 NW 74th Ave, Miami, Florida 33166, USA; or
-Call: 1-868-775-1900

No part of this book may be reproduced or distributed in any form, or by any means, electronic or mechanical – including photocopying, recording, or by any information storage and retrieval system – without the prior written permission of the publisher.

Dedication

To the One I love, my Lord Jesus Christ, this is for You. All that I am and can ever be is because You love me. You have given me wisdom beyond my years, and to serve You is the greatest honour. I could not write this book on my own – it is You who have taught me all that I know. Thank You for choosing me. Thank You for using me. I dedicate this all to You.

Contents

ACKNOWLEDGEMENTS	XI
PREFACE	XII
CHAPTER 1: CAN YOU HEAR HIS CALL?	1
CHAPTER 2: IN SPIRIT AND IN TRUTH	15
CHAPTER 3: COME UP HIGHER	33
CHAPTER 4: THE SACRIFICE OF PRAISE	55
CHAPTER 5: LEARNING TO HEAR GOD'S VOICE	77
CHAPTER 6: FEAR AND FAITH CANNOT MIX	107
CHAPTER 7: THE POWER OF LOVE	125
CHAPTER 8: OBEDIENCE IS BETTER THAN SACRIFICE	145
CHAPTER 9: THE SECRET TO VICTORIOUS LIVING	163

CHAPTER 10: DO NOT FORGET YOUR GOD   177

FINAL WORDS   191

ABOUT THE AUTHOR   193

Acknowledgements

To my mother Althea, you knew that this was a first for me, and when I told you what the Lord had instructed me to do, you never questioned it. You helped me to dream and you stood by me from beginning to end. I thank God that He has blessed me with a mother like you. I love you. Thank you for not giving up on me. Thank you for believing.

My brother Dwight, our conversations about the Lord Jesus and our explorations of doctrine are always exciting. I cannot say that you have not influenced me. Thank you for all that we share.

To every assembly that I have had the privilege of learning and growing in, I say thank you. I have developed very much of who I am today because of my experience with you. The Lord has used our time together to mould and to shape me. Thank you for the important roles that you have played.

To God be the glory!

Preface

I remember when God called me to be a worshipper. I was 25 years old. I had just come off of a high from hosting my very own jazz concert at a local theatre, and from performing at a local jazz festival. There were lovely newspaper articles and reviews. I had received standing ovations and encores. After being a singer and entertainer for most of my life, I thought, "Sure, this would be easy". After all, I have always loved God, and I performed gospel songs as part of my repertoire of jazz, R&B, soul, classical and contemporary. I had even sung in church many a Sunday, and belted out songs of praise in my local choir. When my pastor asked me to join the worship team, I did not hesitate. I thought, "If God could be with me on stage, I could definitely give back to Him in His house. Leading worship would be easy. I'm no stranger to the microphone, I'm a trained, experienced musician; I would love to help out…except on the days when I have my performances". I could not be more wrong.

You see, I came from a background where it was okay to "believe in God" and to live in the world at the same time. It was the norm in my culture (and for the most part, it still is) where to be a "good" Christian (denominational or not) meant that you go to church when you can and do good deeds during the week. You enjoy your life as much as possible, which for me included parties, alcohol, entertainment and enjoying popularity on the social scene, then back to church on the weekend.

I thank God for my foundation in Him as a child, by my parents and grandmother. Looking back now, I see that He has always had His hand upon my life, in every way. And although as a teenager and adult, I had a false perception of what it truly meant to be saved, my heart was always toward Him. So much that even in the midst of a raving nightclub party, my friends would find me in a corner praying. I would always acknowledge God on stage before and/or after every performance. And if there was an altar call at church or at a crusade, the conviction in my human spirit by His Holy Spirit always led me to repentance. I was comfortably having my cake and eating too, while dangerously wearing an undeniable shade of grey. When

Jesus called me and I answered the call, I really had no idea what I said "yes" to.

I unknowingly said "yes" to a complete surrender of my own life to be used by my heavenly Father for His own purpose, for the glory and honour of His name. I said "yes" to the acceptance of God's perfect will, and goodbye to the things of the world. I said "yes" to a process of stripping, moulding, shaping and branding through a fire so hot, that I sometimes could no longer take the pain. I agreed to live a life of holiness and obedience unto God, being led by His Spirit and not after my own desires. I said "yes" to living for Him and having Him live in and through me. I agreed to live in His never-ending love, His emboldening and all-sufficient power and grace, and His beautiful and empowering presence. I said "yes" to living a lifestyle of worship, and I have never looked back.

I have written this book completely by the guidance of the Holy Spirit, and I have learned so very much by what He has revealed to me. It is my intention to share this revelation with you. Each chapter grows in intensity, as you will be taken from milk to meat. I pray that the Holy Spirit will speak to you as you read this book. I promise that it will change your life. It is my hope that you will grow in knowledge, wisdom and understanding, and that you will truly be inspired to live the lifestyle of worship.

God bless you!

Chapter 1

CAN YOU HEAR HIS CALL?

Chapter 1

CAN YOU HEAR HIS CALL?

Every person on this earth has sinned and gone astray, off of God's path and onto our own. We have been led by worldly desires, taught worldly doctrines and fashioned after worldly societies. Most of us have been blinded and moulded by false historical teachings and influenced by corrupt systems of leadership. We live in a dark world that appears to be bright on its surface, but the truth is, we are not meant to remain in that darkness. God is calling His children back to Him. But who are His children?

WHO ARE THE CALLED?

In his address to the Romans of the day, Apostle Paul said, *"For we know that all things work together for good, to them that love God, to them who are **the called,** according to His purpose"* (Romans 8:28. KJV. Emphasis added). I'd like to share the revelation that the Lord gave to me concerning the called, and His children:

"The called, through faith, are the children of Israel. For surely, not all Israel is of Israel, daughter. But, the called, they are My children and heirs to receive My promises. Those who are led by My Spirit, they are the children of the Lord. For I dwell not amongst the children of this world – and not all of mankind are My children. My children are those who receive My Son; they are those who are led by His Spirit, My Spirit – they are the children of Spiritual Israel.

Daughter, although the nation, the geographically central location of the land of Israel truly exists, there is more. There is an Israel of the Spirit – all who are heirs to the promises of Abraham, who live by faith in My Son– they are Spiritual Israel. That is why you are heirs to walk with Him in the new Jerusalem. If Jerusalem was strictly for the Jews of Israel (the *physical nation), then where would My <u>global</u> sons and daughter be?*

Daughter, all who believe in Me, and are led by My great Spirit, they are those who are My children, and thus, heirs to My heavenly kingdom. For I have promised My servant Abraham the <u>nations</u> for children. Not one nation, but many. And yet, I am the Lord God of Israel. Get this clear, My little one, He that keepeth Israel shall neither slumber nor sleep. I am the God of Israel. Over the Promised Land, yes, but also of all heirs of the promise, that is, all Spiritual Israel". (For scriptural reference, read Romans 9:6-8; Romans 8:14, Romans 2:29; 3:29,30; Romans chapter 4, Psalm 121:4).

Did you know that there is an Israel of the Spirit? As we go deeper in this book, you will learn the connection between the spiritual realm and the physical one. But for now, it is important to know that whatsoever happens to Israel in the physical is that which is also happening to it in the spiritual. If you want to have an idea of what may be happening in the Body of Christ, then take note of what is going on in that country and how the world interacts with it. Let us make every effort to be aware of what takes place in Israel, and always include this blessed nation in our prayers, as the Lord has instructed us to do in His Word (Psalm 122:6).

Are you now clear about who are God's called, and who are His children? Can you now confidently say that you are a child of God? Are you amongst His called, heirs to His promises of eternal life with Him, and boldly a part of Spiritual Israel, through your faith in Jesus Christ?

The Bible says, *"Today, if you will hear His voice, harden not your hearts"* (Psalm 95:7). God is calling us out of this world and into His Kingdom. Out of a man-made, Satan-led system of godlessness, where within men's hearts reign the love of money, greed, lust and hatred. Envy, jealousy, sexual impurity and immorality, lies and adultery are seen to be merely *human* traits. Theft, drunkenness, revelry, back-biting, gossip, deceit, murder, fraud, and all manner of filthiness are explained and justified by social and behavioural sciences. God is calling us *out* of a system that declares such acts to be the norm. *Out* of a system which is governed by its own laws and frameworks of morality – that is, "the world"- and into *His* Kingdom (Colossians 1:13). Into His place of dominion, to live in a realm where His perfect law and His Word of righteousness, justice and truth are the commandments that govern men's hearts. A realm where He has the final and only authority, and where He reigns as King of kings and the God of all.

YOU HAVE A CHOICE

The Lord taught me this: the world spins on its own axis, and the beat of the drums of sin is its rhythm. His axis spins oppositely to the direction of the spinning of the world, and so there is fire, sparked by friction. You cannot go both the ways of the world and the ways of the Lord, for they shall overlap and cancel each other. There is clearly friction between the two, and fire to pass through from either side. You have to choose. God says in His Word, that we should not love the world, nor the things of the world, because if we do, then we do not love Him (1 John 2:15).

When we choose God's way, there is no looking back. We cannot mourn for what we left behind: old friends and experiences – the ways of the world. We must set such things behind us, and not be mournful, nor sad, but instead rejoice in the Lord our God who cares for us and will supply all of our needs. That is the high calling to which we have been summoned. One where we wear robes washed white in the blood of the Lamb. One where such robes are unspotted by the mud of the world, and are sanctified and set apart from it. One where we are redeemed from damnation by the saving grace of Jesus Christ our only Saviour, as heirs to the promises of eternal life in Him. A calling to live Spirit-led lives, bringing forth the fruits of righteousness.

THE GREAT SHEPHERD LEADS HIS SHEEP

Jesus called His apostles Peter and Andrew off of their fishing boat, and said to all of His disciples, "Follow Me", and they did. Jesus said, *"No man can come to Me, except the Father who has sent Me draws him"* (John 6:44). Those are the called. He also said, *"My sheep hear My voice, and I know them, and they follow Me"* (John 10:27). Imagine this: five shepherds each own 100 sheep, and at the end of each day, they all gather their respective flocks into one pen to spend the night. One of the shepherds stays behind so that he may stand guard. Five hundred sheep are all gathered together, with no branding or any marks of distinction or identification upon them. Morning comes, bringing with it the four other shepherds. They each set their eyes upon one massive flock. How could they possibly identify their own sheep? How could the sheep know their shepherd, to follow him out from amongst the other sheep? By his voice when he calls them. The Bible says in John 10:3-5, that *"the sheep hear his voice; and he calls his own sheep by name and leads them out. And when he brings out his own sheep, he goes before them; and the sheep follow him, for they know his voice. Yet they will by no means follow a stranger, but will flee from him, for they do not know the voice of strangers*". So it is with the Lord and His own. He calls us all by name from among the people of this world, and we hear Him, obey Him, and follow Him, because He knows us, and we know Him. Jesus is the Great Shepherd. Who are *you* following?

If you think that you are not following anyone, that you are simply living your own life, then you are sadly mistaken. You see, if you are not following the Great Shepherd, whether you realise it or not, whether actively or by default, you are really following the wolf. The enemy of God and man. The accuser, opposer and father of lies, i.e., Satan. It is either one or the other, and it is our decision whom we choose to follow. Whose call are you answering? Have you decided yet? The Lord Jesus expressly said that whosoever is not with Him, is against Him (Luke 11:23). And His Word declares in James 4:4 that the friend of the world is the enemy of God.

We cannot have two masters. We cannot be entangled in the world, and yet be members of Spiritual Israel, confessing Jesus Christ as our Lord and Saviour. By doing this, we bring shame and dishonour to His holy name, automatically become disqualified from being heirs to His promises, and can no longer be called His children. To be a part of this world is to be away from God. To be faithful to the world's system is to live in sin. Sin as we know, is the transgression (breaking) of God's law (1 John 3:4). How can we be governed by God's law of righteousness on one hand, if we are being governed by the laws of a God-less system on the other? There is no dual citizenship with the Almighty God of creation. If we are not in submission to God's laws, then we are not of His Kingdom, and belong not to Him, but to the world, the god of this world being Satan (2 Corinthians 4:4). But God is so loving, merciful and gracious in every possible way, that He has given us the gift of His Holy Spirit to be our counsellor, comforter and guide. To steer us along the right path, conform us into the image of His Son and bring us to His perfect will, for our own good, so that we may partake of His holiness forever through our Lord Jesus Christ.

WHO GOD HAS CALLED, HE HAS PREDESTINED

God calls those whom He has predestined. The holy calling with which He has called us is not according to anything that we could do or accomplish on our own, but according to the *purpose* that He has had, even before the world began (2 Timothy 1:9). He knows the end from the beginning, and what our destinies ought to be, long before we were ever born. Our destinies align with His purpose when we make the decision to answer His call. His Word says that *"Eyes have not seen, nor ears heard, neither has it entered into the hearts of men the things that God has prepared for them that love Him"* (1 Corinthians 2:9). He has plans for us, to prosper us and to give us hope and a bright future. He said, *"Before I formed you in the womb I knew you. Before you were born, I sanctified you"* (Jeremiah 1:5). He chose you long before your very first heartbeat. You must answer His call: seek Him, accept His wonderful Son, Jesus Christ, as your personal Lord and Saviour, submit to Him, love Him and obey Him. It is only then that His Spirit can truly begin to work in you.

Not sure if God's call is upon your life? The fact that you are reading this book is no coincidence. Here is how I realised after some time that God's call was upon my life. You may realise that He is calling you too:

- You find yourself being drawn to the things of God, e.g. His Word, church, repentance.
- You are curious to know who God is.
- You have an unsatisfiable desire to know what your purpose in life is.
- You have a strong drive towards using a gift, talent, skill or ability that you have, for good.
- You believe that there is more to life on earth than what you see and know.
- You believe that there is more to your own life than its current state.
- Opportunities repeatedly come up where people speak God's Word into your life.
- Opportunities arise where you have strange encounters with the supernatural, for example, through dreams, visions, angelic assistance, miracles etc.

I am sure that you are able to relate to at least one of these points. And this list is by no means exhaustive, but I know that by now you have started thinking about God's call.

One thing that is certain is the infallibleness of God's written Word, the Bible, beyond all other ponderings of our own personal inclinations. His Word is the final authority above all else, so I must encourage you to seek God in His Word, and you will find Him, most assuredly.

Unfortunately, many times in searching for answers some of us can end up becoming entangled in false religions and ungodly practices, unknowingly going in the opposite direction to God's voice. As I said earlier, if it is by no other means, we can surely recognize God's voice in His written Word. It is a lamp onto our feet, and a light onto our paths that can and will only lead us along His path of righteousness.

All that we really have to do is surrender to Him. To say, **"Lord Jesus, I want to know You. Please teach me Your way. I want my life to be pleasing to You. Let Your perfect will be done, and not mine. Here I am, please use me. I am Yours"**. A simple prayer of surrender is all it takes for God to begin to work in your life, to break down barriers and walls you thought were impossible to overcome, and to teach you *His* righteousness instead of your own *self-*righteousness. Let Him shape you into the beautiful creation that you were meant to be, no longer disfigured by the world, but transfigured into the image of Christ Jesus. Let Him lead you to live a lifestyle of worship. Will you answer His call?

I would like to ask you another question right now. If you have not yet received Jesus into your heart, are you now ready to become a child of God, to say goodbye to the darkness of this world, and to be translated into God's Kingdom of righteousness, love and light? It is not enough to know *of* Him or to merely acknowledge that He exists. His salvation is a gift that must be personally received (Ephesians 2:8). Let me help you. Firstly, prepare your heart for this decision, then: C.R.C.R. –

Confess your sin. **R**epent of it. **C**onfess Jesus as Lord. **R**eceive Him into your heart.

Pray this prayer of salvation, believe every word with all your heart, and you *will* be saved (Romans 10:9):

"Lord Jesus, I confess that I am a sinner, and that I need a saviour. I am sorry for my sin, and I truly turn away from it today. Please forgive me of all my sins. Lord, I believe that You are the Son of God. Jesus, I believe that you came

from heaven, that you died on the cross, and that you rose from the dead. I believe that you are seated at the right hand of the Father in heaven, and that You will come again. Lord Jesus, I ask You to come into my heart. I receive you as my personal Lord and Saviour. From this day forward, my life is in Your hands. I thank You for the gift of salvation. Amen."

If you prayed this prayer, believe that you have just been born into God's wonderful Kingdom. It is no longer you who live, but Christ now lives in you (Galatians 2:20). Be happy, celebrate and be encouraged, because from now on, your life will never be the same. Praise be to God!

Chapter 2

IN SPIRIT AND IN TRUTH

Chapter 2

IN SPIRIT AND IN TRUTH

I believe that you have decided that you are ready to submit to the perfect will of God for your life. To do so requires setting Him above every other thing, person, relationship or situation. He is now the be all and end all. The first and the last, the beginning and the end, and everything of every moment in between. To answer God's call and to walk in His wisdom and perfect grace, means that we must now worship Him and Him only. We are to have no other gods before Him (Exodus 20:3).

The act of worship, by definition, is the expression of adoration, honour and devotion to a deity, person or thing. But to worship the Lord Jesus Christ goes far beyond the physical action of singing songs of praise, lifting our hands, bowing or kneeling in reverence to His holiness. Though such actions are good, they would mean nothing if the vessels from which the noises are made are unclean.

BODY, SOUL AND SPIRIT: SPIRIT, SOUL AND BODY

When God created Adam, the first man as body, soul and spirit, He breathed His breath of life into Adam and into no other thing that He had created. Everything else was created by God's spoken word. He gave the word and it came forth: light, the sun, moon and stars, land and its creatures, the sea and its creatures. Only into man did God literally breathe *His* very own breath, so that *"man became a living soul"* (Genesis 2:7).

As human beings, we are made up of a physical body, a human soul and a human spirit. The human soul is the life source of our physical existence in the body and is expressed through our fleshly, earthly thoughts, feelings, emotions, personality and character. It is also man's natural sinful nature (Romans 7:18-20). When the physical body dies, so does the soul, and it is then the spirit which remains. The human spirit is the eternal part of our existence, which without spiritual rebirth by faith in Jesus

Christ, it remains fused with our human souls as one. It is the part of our being that has the natural affinity towards the things of God. To the average unbeliever, it would seem difficult to differentiate between the soul and the spirit. That is why our own thoughts, the words that we speak and the things that we do can be so easily corrupted, if we are led by our own spirit (or by an evil spirit) and not by God's Holy Spirit. This is because we are easily influenced by our own experiences, our emotions, our stereotypical mindsets and our own worldly environments. How can we truly worship God if our own spirits are impure? Can anyone truly worship God?

Absolutely. When we accept Jesus Christ as our Lord and Saviour, we receive His Holy Spirit into our own human spirit, and the two merge as one. **We become spiritually reborn.** Take this in slowly: Jesus is the Word (John 1:1). The Word of God is the sword of the Spirit (Ephesians 6:17), which is able to pierce and *divide* soul *and* spirit *and,* it is also a discerner of the thoughts and intentions of the heart (Hebrews 4:12). The Holy Spirit separates the human soul from the human spirit when we accept Jesus as Lord. But what is the adhesive agent between the soul and the spirit that must be severed? It is the mind.

The Bible says in Romans 12:2 *"do not be conformed to this world, but be transformed by the renewing of your mind"*. **What is the mind? It is the inherent portion of one's existence that gives the innate ability to think, reason and process information. It gives way to intellect and depth of thoughtful understanding.** When we are spiritually reborn, our minds must also be renewed, because it is the state of mind which makes the difference between sinful, carnal thinking, and hence behaviour, and godly, Spirit-led thinking, and therefore, behaviour (Romans 8:7). The mind is the link between the human spirit and the soul. Only the Word of God can renew our minds when we commit to obeying it. The Word pierces the mind and brings separation between soulish carnality and godly spirituality.

The mind is one with the heart. **The heart is the natural compass of a man's emotional state, and it is often reflective of the conscious state of mind, whether at a moment in time or over a longer period of time.** The mind *thinks* and the heart *feels*, yet it feels what the mind thinks. Therefore the heart can be likened unto the subconscious mind. Since the Word of God is a discerner of them both, the gash that is formed when they are pierced can only be filled by the Spirit of God. The Word is like a catalyst that fits specifically into the heart that brings about change when the Holy Spirit unites with our spirit and fills the gash.

We no longer are led by our own human lusts and affections, desires and emotions, i.e., the flesh, but by the Spirit of God. That is why the Word of God says that *"As many as are **led** by the Spirit of God, they are the sons of God"* (Romans 8:14. Emphasis added). We become God's children when we have His Spirit dwelling within us, and we become one with Him (1 Corinthians 6:17). For as we know, the body is the temple of the Holy Spirit, and we are therefore no longer our own (1 Corinthians 6:19).

To be a true worshipper of God, we must worship Him in the *spirit,* and not merely with outwardly spoken words or actions. Take a look at this scenario in John chapter 4: 19-24, with Jesus speaking with the woman at the well. It should drive this point home nicely for you:

> *"The woman said to Him, 'Sir, I perceive that You are a prophet. Our fathers worshipped on this mountain, and you Jews say that in Jerusalem is the place where one ought to worship.'*

> *Jesus said to her, 'Woman, believe Me, the hour is coming when you will neither on this mountain, nor in Jerusalem, worship the Father... But **the hour is coming, and now is, when the true worshippers will worship the Father in spirit and truth; for the Father is seeking such to worship Him. God is Spirit, and those who worship Him must worship in spirit and truth.**'"* (Emphasis added).

There are two lessons that will be highlighted here. Firstly, worship is not limited to a place. The Lord Jesus explained to the woman that it mattered not where we worship, for we may not always have a physical place of worship to go to. We are not merely to worship in a building or any designated physical space, because through faith in Jesus Christ, our bodies are already the temples in which God's Spirit dwells. Although He is omnipresent, He is also already inside of us, not in a fixed external location. Our lifestyles must therefore be of reverence to His Lordship.

Secondly, if God's Spirit dwells inside of us, then we can only worship him from the inside out, that is, from one spirit to another, because God *is* Spirit. We cannot merely worship Him with our bodies, nor with only our souls, but with our spirits which are united with His. And that is what

He desires of us: that we honour and love Him with our spirits, and it is this spiritual reverence which will transcend into our emotions (soul) and be demonstrated by our actions (body).

The "truth" that Jesus said we also ought to worship God with is simple: He is the truth, the way and the life (John 14:6). We must follow Him. To live by His truth is to walk in obedience to the perfect will of the Father, as we are led by His Spirit. To walk in His way, is to follow the path that He has set before us, which will lead us to obtaining eternal life by our belief in Him as the Holy Son of God. This is how we will know that we belong to Him, if we believe in Him and if we love one another (1 John 2:3; 3:23). As long as we obey His commandments we can be sure that we are living by the truth and therefore, worshipping in truth.

That was a lot to take in, but there is much more. We have seen that worship begins with our spirit and radiates outwardly into our emotions, thoughts and character (our soul) and then is demonstrated by the things that we say and do (in the body), therefore becoming a lifestyle. However, when we as sinners come to accept the Lord Jesus Christ as our personal God and Saviour, we become newly washed in His blood and redeemed from the penalties of sin. It is up to us to remain that way.

Let me explain: in our newly reborn state, we are basically diamonds in the rough. There is a lot of spiritual dirt and grime that need to be scraped off, and there is a process of refining that we must all go through, so that we may truly begin to live lives that are pleasing to God. As I said earlier, our minds and even our physical lifestyles must be cleaned up and we have to trust God through it all. See here what the Lord shared with me concerning this:

"Think of the diamond, daughter (in its original state). *It is dark and unattractive, not beautiful or brilliant on its own. Can it polish itself? Can it put itself through the refinery, and can it take itself out? Can it turn itself into brilliant beauty and strength that surpass those of any other stone, allowing it to be the most precious amongst the gems of the earth? Does the diamond in the rough not require heat and friction and polishing to shine forth its brilliance? So it is with you, My chosen. I train you up. Depend on Me. Look not to your own self, for you cannot bring forth your own brilliance. I am the Great Jeweler, and you are My diamond. It is only by your faithfulness in Me do I polish and heat and remove the impurities that prevent your shine. For a diamond reflects the*

light around it. If it is I who hold you, whose light will you reflect? Indeed, it is My light. Only I can carry you through the fire and the flame, beat and shave off, purify and shine you. Depend on Me and no other. Stand on My Word and no one else's. Have faith in Me, and I shall cause you to shine as bright as the stars of heaven, for it is My light that shines upon you and from within you." (For scriptural reference, read 1 John 1:5-9, 1 Peter 2:9).

You see now how important it is that we be transformed from dark dullness into pure brilliance, reflecting the righteousness of our God. Only He can get us to where we need to be, because that is what *He* wants for us. We cannot remain the way we once were when we lived in sin, because through the blood of Jesus Christ, we become brand new creations in Him (2 Corinthians 5:17). Old things are passed away. Old habits, old ways of thinking, old ways of speaking, old beliefs, old behaviours, old attitudes, old lifestyles, old stigmas, old labels…old everything, because He makes all things new. He transforms us when we submit to His Lordship and allow the Holy Spirit to work in us, to rearrange our former worldly selves into a godly image, i.e., His image. It is therefore impossible to become a child of God and yet remain unchanged.

THE KEY TO TRANSFORMATION

The key therefore is repentance: sincere remorse for our sin, which leads to the conscious decision and commitment to turn away from it and not return to it again. Repentance is not committing the same sin over and over again, because we believe that God will always forgive us. That is perpetual sin, which God does not endorse. When we receive Jesus as our Lord and Saviour, we commit to living lives of holiness unto Him, because according to Apostle Peter, *"as He who has called you is holy, you also be holy in **all** your conduct"* (1 Peter 1:15. Emphasis added). We must earnestly try to think, speak, act and do the things that we think that Jesus would, all for the glory of His name. We must endeavour to stay away from the things which we know that He would disapprove of, for the sake of our own salvation, and also so that we do not dishonour Him. This of course, can only happen when we really get to know Jesus by spending time with Him. We will examine this later on.

Know however, that temptations will come. There *is* an enemy who does not want to lose his grasp on your life, and will do his best to frustrate your effort of changing your life from worldliness to holiness. Yet, be comforted that without a doubt, you are not on your own. God gives us the grace to overcome all manner of temptation, through Jesus our Lord. He was tempted in all areas that we are, yet He did not sin (Hebrews 4:15). He is our example of overcoming the world. If He did it, then by His enabling Holy Spirit which we all possess, surely we can overcome the world too. He equips us to do that which is beyond our own natural capabilities, sets us apart from sin, and never allows us to be tempted beyond that which we are able, but instead, always makes a way of escape for us (2 Corinthians 10:13). This is the essence of His grace.

If you ever find that although you have accepted Jesus Christ as Lord, and you still live the same way that you used to, still think, speak and act the way that you used to, then the problem is not Him, it's you. Something is either knowingly or unknowingly keeping you from experiencing the grace that ought to transform you. What can you do? One approach is this: ask the Lord to change you into the person that He created you to be, that you no longer be the person who you once were before you knew Him. David's Psalms display a tremendous array of human experiences in pursuit of God's holiness. God's Word is there to encourage, strengthen, wash us and cleanse us that He may work in us and through us. You can certainly pray the way that David did. Here are two of many of his earnest prayers:

Psalm 19: 13-14:
"Cleanse me from secret faults. Keep back Your servant also from presumptuous sins; let them not have dominion over me. Then I shall be blameless, and I shall be innocent of great transgression. Let the words of my mouth and the meditation of my heart be acceptable in Your sight, O Lord, my strength and my Redeemer."

And also Psalm 51:1-12:
"Have mercy upon me, O God, according to Your lovingkindness; according to the multitude of Your tender mercies, blot out my transgressions. Wash me thoroughly from my iniquity, and cleanse me from my sin. For I acknowledge my transgressions and my sin is always before me. Against You, You only, have I sinned, and done this evil in Your sight—that You may be found just when You speak, and blameless when You judge. Behold, I was brought forth in iniquity, and in sin my mother conceived me. Behold, You desire truth in the inward

parts, and in the hidden part You will make me to know wisdom. Purge me with hyssop, and I shall be clean; wash me, and I shall be whiter than snow. Make me hear joy and gladness, that the bones You have broken may rejoice. Hide Your face from my sins, and blot out all my iniquities. Create in me a clean heart, O God, and renew a steadfast spirit within me. Do not cast me away from Your presence, and do not take Your Holy Spirit from me. Restore to me the joy of Your salvation, and uphold me by Your generous Spirit." Amen.

In repenting of our sins, we should henceforth desire and strive to have clean hands (be upright in what we do and say) and pure hearts (have clean thoughts, motives and intentions). That is the only way that we may ascend to God's holy place, having been washed by the blood of Jesus (Psalm 24: 3-5). And if you have any doubt concerning where God is and what He sees, know that according to Psalm 11:4, *"the Lord is in His holy temple, the Lord's throne is in heaven; His eyes behold, His eyelids test the sons of men."* We can never ascend to such a holy, awesome God with dirty minds. What's in your mind? What fills your thoughts? Whatever it is, know that according to God's Word, we ought to think on whatsoever is true, honest, respectful, pure, lovely, good, morally upright and praiseworthy, and we ought to trust and believe that we have the mind of Christ. (Philippians 4:8, 1 Corinthians 2:16) We ought to be able to know that which is God's will for us, through revelation by His Holy Spirit. That means that wicked thoughts, feelings of hatred, bitterness, malice, anger, unforgiveness, jealousy, envy, pride and perversions have no place in us as children of God. Committing ungodly acts of theft, fraud, lying, fornicating, gluttony, gossip, backbiting, showing favouritism, racism, violence, speaking foul language, and the sort, should no longer be carried out in our flesh. As we seek to be holy, as He who has called us is holy, we truly begin to walk in alignment with His will for our lives. By His Spirit, we are led away from our sinful nature, and into His righteousness. That is how we may truly worship the Lord with our lives.

THREE HEAVENS

Allow me to share another revelation that the Lord gave to me concerning the body, soul and spirit of man in relation to the three heavens. Imagine that you are standing outdoors and you look up to the sky. Firstly, you see the natural light of the sun in our blue skies above the earth (the stratosphere), and in looking further beyond that sky, you see the darkness of outer space, but looking even beyond that outer darkness, you see the spiritual light of heaven. Three layers, three heavens, three realms. Here's the revelation, remembering that God is tripartite:

"The natural light represents the flesh. The light of the earth is the light that is seen of men. What you do (in the body) *resonates and reflects light around you like a mirror. That is why what you do defines your character in the eyes of men.*

The darkness (cosmos) *represents the human spirit devoid of My presence.* (It is both a physical realm and a spiritual realm, because it is there where the outcasts of heaven dwell, also known as the second heaven.) *For I am the light of the world. I am the light that illuminates the soul. Therefore My Spirit burns within you like the sun, keeping you in orbit. The fire that burns consumes. It gives life. I burn like the sun within you, daughter. When you see My light in the eyes of a man, you see it shine through his works. Therefore, let My light shine through you. Shine My light by the fire of My Spirit.*

The spiritual light above (the third heaven) *is the light of My Kingdom, deep within the spirit of a man. Daughter, for as it is in heaven, so on earth; as in the spirit, then in the natural; as it is in the inner spirit of a man, so it is in the manifestation of his flesh. The Kingdom of God dwells within the hearts of men. The Word of the Lord your God in the spirit of a man. My light shines into the darkness, it burns like the sun to illuminate the soul and shines through the flesh, through the works of a man – body, soul and spirit."* (For scriptural reference read 2 Corinthians 12:2, Psalm 148:4, Matthew 5:16, Luke 17:21, John 8:12).

What a revelation. There is so much depth there. I hope that you will ask the Lord to reveal to you even more from what you just read. There is more to us as human beings than we often realise, and our existence has been completely designed by a totally tripartite God – Father, Son and Spirit (1 John 5:7). As He is holy, as three in one, so must we be holy, in body, soul and spirit. May we shine as a beacon to the lost wherever the Lord sends us, that His name may be glorified through our lives.

Chapter 3

COME UP HIGHER

Chapter 3

COME UP HIGHER

We have been called out of this world to a divine purpose. Out of darkness, obscurity and uncertainty, and into the marvelous light of our one true living God. We are no ordinary people. We are a chosen generation, sanctified by God. We are a holy nation. A royal priesthood. A peculiar people (1 Peter 2:9). We have the Spirit of the Almighty God of all creation living inside of us, making us supernatural in every way. We have the capacity to come up higher into an increased consciousness and understanding of the things of God, taught to us by the Spirit of God, that only those born of His Spirit can ever possibly comprehend (1 Corinthians 2:10-16).

God has called us higher, and He has equipped us with the gifts and the talents that we need for the road that He has called us onto. For not only are we now His children, but we are also His servants, given assignments to be carried out on the earth, in Jesus' name. We are no longer people of earth working our way into God's Kingdom, but in fact, we are people of God's Kingdom carrying out His will on the earth. Our individual paths may be different, but our goal the same: to bring glory and honour to His name through the quality of our lives, fulfilling His purpose upon the earth.

STAY FOCUSED

In our transition from being children of darkness into becoming children of light, there is never an easy road. Trials, temptations, tests and hardships will come. Even persecution will come from both strangers and loved ones (2 Timothy 3:12). But no matter the tumult of the waves of the tongues of men, we are to keep our focus on our Lord Jesus Christ. To keep our eyes fixed on Him through faith in His Word, setting our eyes on heavenly things which we can only see in the spirit, and not upon things on the earth that we see with our physical eyes. This is absolutely necessary if we are to be qualified as servants of God. We cannot afford to become distracted.

What would you say is a distraction? **It is any thing, person, activity or situation that draws your attention away from what God has called you to do.** Distractions can come in any form. Know this: if it takes you away from your assignment, it is a distraction. If it takes up most of your time, in that you have none for the Lord, it is a distraction. If you cannot concentrate on His Word or His mission, you are being distracted. We are to stay clear of distractions if we are to live purposeful lives for our Lord Jesus Christ.

Do you remember the account of Apostle Peter and the Lord Jesus, when they both walked on water? (Matthew 14:22-33). Such waters were not calm, but rough. No still, quiet waters, but raging, frothy, tumultuous waves. Those waves are likened unto the hardships of life: sudden changes, mockers, scoffers and scornful men, hurtful words spoken and trying times (Isaiah 57:20). Rough waters. When you find that the Lord has called you out of your boat to charter a new course, pioneering in the faith for His Kingdom, the only thing that you may have sometimes, is faith. Like Peter, God often calls us out into tumultuous waves so that we may trust Him with our lives. As I mentioned in Chapter 1, is He not our Shepherd? If a sheep is afraid of its shepherd, will it trust him? No, but it will run away from him. Don't be afraid of Jesus. He knows us better than we know our own selves. He knows our strengths, weaknesses and capabilities, and will never ask us to do what we are unable to do. We are to fear the Lord, yes, with reverend love, honour, obedience and respect, but not as though He were a hostile slave driver or cruel master. He is not. He is love (1 John 4:16). He will always be there for us, to protect us with His very own life! Don't run way when He calls you out to meet Him in waters that appear to be vicious. Trust that He will carry you across those waters safely. Trust that it is He and He alone who is your guide, and that by faith in Him, earnest, deep and sincere trust in Him, you *will* accomplish that which He has called you out to do.

The key to success above all else, is to keep your eyes fixed on Him. Spend time reading God's Word and believing what the Lord says in His Word, no matter how things may appear. Trust that His Word is true, and that He is faithful to do exactly what He says that He would. Remember the godly, encouraging words spoken over your life by others, and declare them boldly out of your own lips. Confess God's will for your life and trust that He will bring it to pass. He is our counsellor and He is our guide. He is our teacher, our helper, our healer, our protector, our provider and our strength. He is our Father, and He is our friend. Though there be harsh winds, thunder and lightning, and it seems like you may be overwhelmed by the roughness of the waves, never become distracted. Instead, trust the Lord. The moment we give in to distractions, we lose sight of Him and His purpose for our lives. We cease to hear His voice clearly, we come out of His portal of grace, and we sink into the waters of doubt. Be careful, lest you drown.

Distractions can also come in the various cares of this life. A distraction can come in the form of a desirable gift. It can either be tangible or intangible, such as a sponsored opportunity or luxury from a colleague or associate. There is also the possible distraction of a seemingly charming person who enters into your life and grabs your attention. Do yourself a favour and before you accept any gift or new person into your life, seek the Lord's counsel so that you may know whether or not it is His doing. For gifts are usually given with a particular motive, whether pure or corrupt, and can leave you bound to its giver, should you receive it. And persons in your life who are not sent by God, may subtly be used by Satan, whether knowingly or unknowingly, to cleverly pull you away from advancing God's Kingdom. Desire the gift of wisdom, which God gives freely to all those who ask Him, (James 1:5) and understanding, that you may know what His perfect will is.

SPIRITUAL SUPERPOWERS

As a believer in Jesus Christ, the Creator of the universe and the power source of all things that exist, (Colossians 1:16,17) we are given the tremendous privilege of being transformed into His image, by His Holy Spirit. When Jesus walked among men, He performed some of the most mind shattering miracles ever seen, most of them personal, and in great masses. Yet, He said to His disciples:

> *"Most assuredly, I say to you, he who believes in Me, the works that I do he will do also; and greater works than these he will do, because I go to My Father. And whatever you ask in My name, that I will do, that the Father may be glorified in the Son. If you ask anything in My name, I will do it".* (John 14:12)

What does that mean? It means that we can do it too. The Lord Jesus gave us the authority to heal all manner of sickness and disease, to cast out devils and to raise the dead. He gave us the authority to crush serpents, scorpions and all the power of the devil beneath our feet, with the assurance that nothing shall by any means hurt us, by His blood, and in His Name (Matthew 10:1, 8; Luke 10:19). We are not normal.

In living lifestyles of worship unto the Lord, He equips us all with the spiritual gifts that are necessary for the successful completion of the specific tasks assigned to each and every one of us. Imagine a video game where you start at level one with the basic tools that you need to overcome the obstacles in your way. With each new level that you get to, the challenges get harder and your enemies get bigger as you move closer to conquering your quest. There are tokens along the way to aid in your success, and it is up to you to know how well to use them. So it is with us. Each gift is for a purpose towards our destinies in Christ, to be used for His glory. According to Apostle Paul, the Holy Spirit gives us: the word of wisdom, the word of knowledge, faith, prophecy, healing, the working of miracles, the gift of speaking in tongues, the interpretation of tongues, and the discerning of spirits. And He gives them out as He sees fit (1 Corinthians 12:7-11). However, we must first desire them, for truly they are within us by His Spirit, by His power and awesome grace, but we must use our willpower. This must not be for our own selfish ambition, to boast or to appear to be more "blessed" than others, because the Lord knows our hearts. It is He who will give us a particular desire in alignment with the tasks that He has laid out for us on the earth, for the glory of His Kingdom. We must therefore spend time in His Word, learning more of who our God is, and the context in which to use these gifts. When the Lord put the desire in me for His spiritual gifts, He said these things to me:

- *"You want to heal by My Spirit? You must be pure, and your heart and hands must be clean (you must forgive!).*
- *Prophecy requires a clean mind.*
- *When you speak and hear others speak* (in tongues), *listen to the voice of My Spirit. He will reveal all interpretation to you.*
- *Miracles come by My Blessed Spirit, as He wills it to be. You must be covered by My holy anointing through worship. Worship is more than an art, it is a lifestyle.* **You must live a life of worship.**

- *Faith demonstrates. Not only is it to be preached of, but to be demonstrated. The more you demonstrate your belief in Me, the greater your faith."*

We see that it is absolutely essential to live a lifestyle of worship. God should not only find us ready to receive His gifts, but He should also be able to use us to have an eternal impact on the lives of others by the use of those gifts. We must therefore be responsible stewards with whichever gifts that we have been given by the Lord for our life's journey. We must never neglect them, but continue in our obedience and worship of the Lord, that they may grow (1 Timothy 4:14). For their purpose is not for our own gloating, celebration or flaunting, but for *service* – working to help the Body to grow and develop according to the plans and the purposes of God. Therefore be content and diligent to nurture and develop the gifts that the Lord gives to you, and don't be jealous or envious of anyone else's spiritual gifts, talents or abilities. What one person has been called to do is different to what the Lord has called another to do. But together, abilities combined, both persons may be a tremendous force against the kingdom of darkness, by the power of the Spirit of God.

WITH GREAT POWER COMES GREAT RESPONSIBILITY

To be clear, we have no spiritual power of our own. It is God's power in us that enables us to live victorious lives through our Lord Jesus Christ (Acts 3:12-15; Zechariah 4:6). However, when He chooses to bless us with the gifts of His Holy Spirit, know that we will be held responsible for what we do with them. For whether we continue to live holy lifestyles or not, God will not take back His gifts or His calling, (Romans 11:29) but we will have to answer in the day of judgement for what we have done with them and with our lives (2 Corinthians 5:10; Revelation 20:11-15).

It is important therefore that we remain humble at all times. That is the key to never falling into the enemy's deception - into believing that it is we who can perform great works and do miraculous signs and wonders of our own selves. That is a dangerous trap which Satan uses, so that you may come out of God's alignment, and lose your anointing (divine commission and demonstration of God's power in His presence). Satan does this so that you may become a pawn that he can use to carry out his own vile purposes. Should this happen, he will use the gifts that *God* once gave to you for *His* divine purpose, for his own deceitful acts of rebellion, witchcraft, divination and those of other demonic influences. The good thing is that we know the root of this deception, and it is **pride**.

The Lord taught this to me:

*"Leaven in the heart of a man is but a heavy weight to his spirit. For though he is inflated in his own eyes, he is weighed down and unable to ascend, not only to My calling, but to My presence. Pride keeps a man from kneeling before the Lord, your God. Pride causes the knees of men to be broken by the God of Power and Might. For at the sound of My name, **every** knee shall bow, and **every** tongue shall confess that I am the God of Salvation. All men, all of creation shall bow down to Me. Pride stiffens the neck and hardens the heart. Pride keeps a man from knowing the great love of his Maker, but keeps not the Maker from displaying His power.*

Daughter, I tell you these things to teach you about the spirit of pride. For pride is paired with insecurity. Insecurity comes with envy and jealousy. Jealousy comes with murder and lust. Lust comes with covetousness and discontentment. Know these well, for the spirit of pride acts not alone. It is too proud to be by itself; it desires company. How can one be prideful without an audience?

So you see, My child, I teach you what are the characteristics and spiritual consequences of pride. Pride is that spirit that controlled the heart of Satan against Me. Pride: love of self above all others, where every other being is seen as subservient to the prideful one. Now you know about the spirit of pride. Let not such a spirit enter into you through the presence of its accompanying spirits.

Remain humble before me at all times, and I will lift you up. Do you see why the humble are exalted? They are like hot air balloons. The emptier you are of yourself, the more My Spirit can fill you, and you become lifted higher by My grace. The proud are cast down because they are too heavily filled with the cement of self." (For scriptural reference, read Philippians 2:10,11, Proverbs 29:23, James 4:6, 1 John 2:16).

The "cement of self": hard, porous, arid and heavy. May we never be so filled with our own selves that our Lord cannot lift us up to bring forth His glory. We see that being filled with one's self is not merely a flaw in character. It is the demonstration of demonic presence within the life of the proud one. It is a spirit that must be bound and cast out in

Jesus' mighty name. When we recognize the issue of pride in our hearts, we must firstly repent of it, and its associated colleagues, and seek to be completely delivered from them all by the power of the Holy Spirit. However, as much as we may cut off the branches of pride through repentance and submission to God, even by fasting and praying, we will find that we cannot truly be rid of that stubborn, insubordinate demon unless it is fully uprooted from where it is deeply buried. **Pride does have a root, and its root is insecurity and the fear of being looked down upon.**

The Holy Spirit taught me that when you are insecure about yourself, the words and actions of others offend you. It can be the simplest thing that someone does or says that you perceive to be disrespectful, rude, offensive or even hurtful. You may not have recognized it before, but you have hidden insecurities. We all do. Search yourself, and meditate on this. You may be insecure about your position in society, your level of accomplishment or your financial situation. You may be insecure about your body image, physical stature, your background or beginnings, your skillfulness or limited capabilities. You become insecure about how you are perceived by others, and you begin to fear being looked down upon by them. To counteract this, you *exalt* an image of yourself to others, which you expect *them* to live up to. You expect people to treat you a certain way, according to how you perceive your own self. If they do not interact with you according to your own standard or expectation, then you feel slighted, offended, disrespected. Pride has stepped in.

There is a level of respect and honour that everyone deserves, but no one is obligated to treat you the way you think that you deserve to be treated. When you are secure in your identity in Jesus Christ, in who *He* says that you are, you have peace in the inner man, and the outward perceptions of the people around you become meaningless. You find yourself in Him, and not in the opinions of others. Therefore external treatment from others becomes less personally offensive. You are able to be resilient in the face of criticism, and even when experiencing real dishonour or disrespect, you will be able to respond thoughtfully, rather than react emotionally.

Insecurity and the fear that opens the door to pride, are deeply rooted and often begin in our childhood or early years. They are strongholds that Satan has set up to keep us in bondage as we mature. These strongholds must be torn down (2 Corinthians 10: 3-5), so that the Lord may begin to work in us, as we cast our cares upon Him, and trust Him to deliver us from the hand of the enemy. Ask the Lord to reveal to you exactly what your hidden insecurities and fears are, so that you may repent of them, and truly become delivered from that deceitful spirit of pride.

FRUIT LABELS

Living the lifestyle of worship requires sowing good seeds and reaping good fruit. In this light, I will only highlight the importance of our behaviour as representatives of Christ. There is a saying that "your life may be the only Bible that some people will ever read". What influence are you having on the people around you? Are you leading others toward Christ, or causing them to run away from both Him and yourself?

As diamonds from the Kingdom, the light which we should reflect must be the light of the One who holds us. This is how we will be identified in this world. Not by what we do and say for others to see and hear, but when no one else is watching. Do our nice words line up with our actions? Do our kind actions reflect our real feelings? Let us not be hypocrites. Instead, let us yield to the Holy Spirit, who will teach us how to walk in true love, real joy and pure peace. He alone can teach us enduring patience, sincere kindness, godly goodness, solid faithfulness, caring gentleness and matured self-control (Galatians 5:22,23). When we bear such godly fruit, we honour the One who has called us to be His ambassadors.

GOOD FRUIT. BAD FRUIT.

When the Lord Jesus taught His disciples how to identify hypocrites and frauds, He said that *"by their fruits, you shall know them"* (Matthew 7:16-20). That is, the true identity of a person is revealed through his/her lifestyle, whether godly or worldly, sincere or pretentious. What we produce defines who we really are. This also applies to the Body of Christ, including apostles, prophets, evangelists, pastors and teachers, as well as ministry workers, congregational members and everyone else who confesses Jesus Christ as Lord. Let us therefore be vigilant to examine our intentions and our motives, and be wise to those of other individuals within our spheres of influence. Let us not be as they who do the works of the Kingdom merely for men's eyes to see, but whose hearts are not toward the Lord God. Instead, their eyes are toward their own gain, their own fame, and human accolade. Let us ensure that our actions line up with our sweet words and pleasant teachings (Romans 2:21-24). Look at the company that you keep and the way in which you carry yourself. Take a look at the way in which you operate, in deed and in speech. Do you do what is right? Do those around you do the same?

Know that not everyone who shows up to minister with mighty signs and wonders are the servants of God. If they carry not God's glory (see Chapter 9), then they are not God's servants, but instead of their father the devil, operating with counterfeit spiritual "power". Discern the purity and sincerity of men's hearts, for the heart is the dwelling place of the Spirit of God. An impure heart usually lacks the presence of the Spirit, and spews forth defilements out of the mouth, often hidden behind admirable actions (Matthew 12: 34, 35). We must not be blinded by flashing lights in this world: those proclaiming the Kingdom of God, yet whose offices are set up in the kingdom of darkness – false lights. Dark lights appearing to be bright, purposed to blind the eyes of those unknowing. By their fruits you shall know them. There are many false shepherds and many sheep that are devoured by wolves in disguise. Discern the right. We must not be too quick to jump at every "Christian" missionary or five-fold leader (Ephesians 4:11). For many ministers of Satan disguise themselves amongst God's flock and blind the eyes of the unwise. They speak sweet words of deception, which come out of their mouths like thick black smoke over the people. That darkness turns the bright eyes of the people black, until they do not even recognise their own blindness. The light that they see in that state is dark light, and only the truth of Jesus Christ can shatter their tainted lenses. Satan even disguises himself as an angel of light to draw you into his darkness (2 Corinthians 11:14). Therefore test the spirits that surround you, whether they be of Christ, speaking the complete truth of the Gospel and telling no lies, boldly confessing the Lordship of Jesus in actions, words and behaviour (1 John 4:1-3). May we seek to produce the fruits of the righteousness of our God, not operating out of our own self-will but at all times and in all things, giving honour unto our Lord Jesus through the quality of our lives.

THE QUALITY OF A MAN

There is no hiding it: a righteous man does righteous deeds, because He serves a righteous God (1 John 3:7, 10). I would like to share the revelation that the Lord gave to me concerning the quality of a man:

"Does the movement of the pen determine the quality of the words that are written? (Here I answered, 'No, Lord') *You are right, My chosen, for no matter the appearance of the word, or the language in which it is written, its quality belongs only with its inner meaning. So it is with the servants of God. It matters not the appearance of a man, his height nor his stature. The quality of a man begins with his inner nature. No matter the outer man, the quality of a man lies on the inside: in his spirit man. Whether or not the spirit man is of good or bad quality, depends only upon the man in which he dwells. For the physical man relies upon his soul. If the spirit be not nourished by My Word, the quality of a man would be very little.*

Time in My Word causes growth in the quality of your spirit. As your spirit develops and grows into an adult, so will My Spirit within you interact with you in like manner. If you be but a babe, then My Spirit will treat you, and interact with, and teach you as a babe. An adolescent, as an adolescent, an adult as an adult. Time in My Word transforms the heart, shapes the conscience and transforms the spirit from a caterpillar into a butterfly. Only I can do this, for I the Lord do witness the inner quality of a man. Dear daughter, it matters not the outside of a man, it is the quality of his spirit is that which makes a man a good servant of the living God. Be not deceived nor misled to judge a man by his outer looks only – look at the quality of his spirit." (For scriptural reference, read 1 Samuel 16:7).

Therefore it matters not who we appear to be on the outside, in the sight of other people's eyes. God sees the heart. He knows our inner emotions, our secret desires, our thoughts, our motives and our intentions. We cannot fool Him. We cannot hide anything from Him. Let this be a lesson for us all, that we may not mislead nor be misled by others flaunting a sanctimonious lifestyle, only to be seen in God's eyes as a white-washed tomb. God forbid.

As His Word says, *"Do not be deceived, God is not mocked; for whatever a man sows, that he will also reap"* (Galatians 6:7). As we seek to grow and to come up higher in the holy calling of our Lord Jesus Christ, may we seek to sow seeds of the righteousness of God, that we may reap the pleasant fruits of His Holy Spirit.

Chapter 4

THE SACRIFICE OF PRAISE

Chapter 4

THE SACRIFICE OF PRAISE

Hallelujah! Glory be to the only living God. The God who was and is and who forevermore shall be. Almighty, omnipotent, omnipresent, omniscient, gracious and glorious and righteous and just and true! Marvellous in word and deed! Yeshua, the great and Holy One, be glorified and exalted forever and ever, upon the earth and in all the heavens! Hallelujah! All hail King Yeshua, the righteous! Yeshua, the glorious One! Praise Him forevermore!

WHY WE PRAISE

We praise the Lord because He is good and because His mercy endures forever (Psalm 118:1). Praise is a vital component of the lifestyle of worship. Praise not only establishes Jesus' Lordship over our lives, but it is also a mighty weapon against the enemy. It is the declaration of the glory, power and goodness of God because He is God. *"It is He who has made us, and not we ourselves"* (Psalm 100:3). As believers in the Lord Jesus Christ, praise forms a part of our everyday lives. We ought to praise the Lord for all things, in all things and through every circumstance, for He is still our God.

Praise is also a fundamental pillar in the *act* of worshipping our Lord. It is the key that unlocks the door to His presence. The greatest of all psalmists, King David prophetically said these words: *"Open to me the gates of righteousness; I will go through them,* **and** *I will praise the Lord. This is the gate of the Lord, through which the righteous shall enter"* (Psalm 118: 19, 20. Emphasis added). The Lord gave me this revelation of that Scripture:

"The gate of the righteousness of the Lord your God is not a metaphor, My daughter. It is My holy temple. You must enter into My courts with thanksgiving and praises unto the Lord Most High. The unrighteous stand outside. There is no sound from the dry bones of the unrepentant sinner. But the righteous, they shall enter through My gate. The righteous shall come into My courts, for I open the gates of My temple to the righteous. My daughter, for the unrighteous shall stand before Me in the day of judgement, but they shall not stand in the congregation of the righteous. The righteous are My faithful servants – the faithful saints of God, whom I shall open the gates of My courts to. That is why you enter in with thanksgiving and with praises. For not every soul enters My courts. Those who enter in are the ones whom I have called – My children. Are you not My own child? The children of the Lord come into His gates. The saints shall pass through this gate into My courts. You shall not remain outside. Come inside! I open the gates to you. This is the gate of the Lord. Your name is in My book of life. Enter into My courts with praise. This is the gate through which the righteous shall enter." (For scriptural reference, read Ezekiel 43-46, Psalm 11:4, Psalm 100:4, Matthew 7:13,14, Psalm 1: 5, Revelation 20:12,13).

Who can say that they have been through these gates without worship? Who can say that they have seen the glory of

God beyond the law of righteousness? (Romans 3:20-22). None shall ascend to the hill of the Lord if they be unclean, as we saw in Chapter 2. Shall we enter into His courts as unrepentant sinners? Never. We enter into His courts with praise, for we enter into His realm of light and peace, where there is joy in His presence. Without praise, shall the gate be opened? I think not. It is essential for our relationship with God that we praise Him, so that we may begin to see the manifestation of His glory in our lives, that is, His power, His presence and His perfect love which completes us. In looking at the temple of God, as we see with King Solomon's temple (1 Kings 6; 2 Chronicles 3), and Moses' tabernacle (Exodus 39:32-43), when one enters through the gate, a sacrifice is brought to be offered unto the Lord. In these times, where our bodies are the actual temples of the Holy Spirit in this earthly plane, we enter in through the gates of righteousness with the sacrifice of praise.

What is the sacrifice of praise? It is an offering of praise that one gives to the Lord when there is nothing more precious that can be given to Him. It is the dedicated commitment to praising the Lord not only for what He has done in our lives, but for who He is, regardless of our circumstance. For although tangible offerings of our financial increase are pleasing to Him (with the right motives and intentions), it is our praise that reaches God in His own inner being, as we praise Him not merely with spoken words, but with our spirit to His Spirit. It is not the quantity of an offering that the Lord sees, but instead, how much it costs. This applies both in the spiritual sense and in the physical sense. If it costs you nothing to give, then it is worth nothing to God. When it costs you something, it comes from the heart, and it is that which moves God – the heart condition.

How much does it cost you to offer praise to the Lord when you are feeling lost or broken? What does it cost you to praise Him when you are hurt, sick, in mourning, depressed or in despair? I am sure that it costs everything that you have, because I can say that it is not easy to praise the Lord when life is not going well. It is not easy to praise Him when you do not feel like it, have no zeal to do so, feel like you cannot face Him or do not know what to say. And that is when praise becomes sacrificial. When we lift our hands that seem to be filled with lead: that is when praise becomes a sacrifice. When we look around us and do not know what to do, and it would be easier to give up or to turn back. When we would just rather hide, yet find the courage to stand and declare that Jesus is King, He is the Lord our God, and He is greater than our situation – that is the sacrifice of praise.

PRAISE BRINGS FOCUS. PRAISE BRINGS PEACE.

When we give praises unto God, we set our eyes upon Him, and every distraction melts away into oblivion. Tumultuous waves may be roaring and noisy winds may be blowing, but when we declare the Lordship of Jesus Christ in our lives, who else's face can we behold before us, but His? He fills us with the power of His Holy Spirit and the boldness and confidence to declare in His name, "Peace, be still!". And that is the key to withstanding trial and to overcoming every test in this life– the declaration of Jesus' goodness, His power and His might! Only then can we hear His voice clearly and receive direction, counsel, strategy, guidance and instructions from Him, by His Spirit.

I remember when the Lord was taking me through a period of refining and training, I passed through so many hardships. It was such a challenge for me at the time. Very often throughout that two year period, I felt like if I was nothing. I had no friends, no job, no success in my business, no social life and no money. I often got a hard time even at church, my family had problems with relatives, and doors were being shut in every direction. Worry, stress and anxiety plagued me. I could not stop complaining about how challenging my life seemed to be. But the more that I complained, the more difficult things became, and I seemed to be nearly stagnant in my spiritual growth. When things got too hard to bear, I just could not find the strength or the zeal to praise God. My prayers were instead filled with whining and complaints. I never stopped believing that God was there for me, yet I was too busy feeling sorry for myself to be aware of His presence in my life. Too often I had lost sight of Him, and the enemy had me just where he wanted me – in a place of self-defeat and spiritual deafness. I could not hear God's voice clearly, and I was awfully confused. I thank God that He never gave up on me, and that He gave me His grace to get through it all. He showed me that I needed to have an **attitude of praise**. *"Praise Me in the midst of the storm"*, He said to me. I obeyed Him, and that is when everything changed.

When I began to offer God the sacrifice of praise, I did it many times with a heavy heart and with tear-filled eyes. But by the time I would be finished, my tears would be gone, and my spirit lifted. His Spirit would comfort me and strengthen me, teach me what to say and even how to pray. At times when I could not find words, He would pray through me. I began to trust Him more and my faith increased. He taught me that it is in Him I live, in Him I breathe, and in Him I have my being (Acts 17:28). Nothing on earth could sustain me besides His love. Having an attitude of praise, declaring the power, majesty and the love of my Lord Jesus granted me peace, and allowed the Holy Spirit to move powerfully in my life. I became delivered from anxiety, worry and fear. Human interactions became simpler and life seemed easier to bear. I began to grow quite rapidly in my spirit, as I would draw nearer to God in His Word and in prayer, and He began to draw nearer to me (James 4:8).

I have shared this because I know that someone reading this will be able to relate to my experience and be encouraged to praise the Lord. In hard times, praise Him. In difficult times, praise Him. In anger and in hurt, in struggle and in lack, in confusion and dismay and when trouble is the norm, praise the Lord, even in the midst of the storm. He is our strength, our protector, our provider and our peace. Let me share what the Lord Jesus taught to me about peace:

"Peace begets restfulness of body, mind and soul, and the spirit takes ease to worship and to listen to My voice. I give you the peace of My Spirit. Understand what I say, My daughter. The peace of God surpasses and extends beyond the logic of man. Peace says safety in the midst of trial. Peace says freedom in the tails of bondage. Peace says joy in the midst of sorrow. Peace in Me says that you are unfazed by your surrounding circumstances and environment, for your faith and your hope are anchored in the Lord, your God. My daughter, peace is most precious, and it far outweighs the knowledge and the understanding of mankind, who can know no peace.

My peace I give unto you. With the peace of the Lord comes the fulfilment of purpose and the freedom from envy, all carnality and all distraction. Peace says to the storm 'be still'. Peace says to the waves, 'do not shake, nor rise up'. Peace says to the running waters 'be slow, be quiet'. Be glad, dear daughter, and begin to operate truly from a peaceful heart, mind and spirit. I am with you always. Know My peace. For I am with you, and I am the God of peace." (For scriptural reference, read John 14:27, Philippians 4:7, Judges 6:24, Isaiah 9:6).

When I surrendered my life completely into Jesus' beautiful hands and found my safety and strength in His presence, I chose to praise Him. I made a choice to obey Him and to trust Him, and He granted me His peace. If you want the peace of the Lord in your life, make the choice to praise Him today.

PRAISE DEFEATS THE ENEMY

As it is in heaven, so it is manifested on earth. As it is in the spiritual realm, so it is manifested in the natural. There is an enemy who lurks about like a roaring lion seeking whom he may devour (1 Peter 5:8). There is an enemy whose sole purpose is to steal, to kill and to destroy the children of God (John 10:10). He hates us with perfect hatred and will stop at nothing to see us separated from God because of sin, and cast into hell to be tortured for eternity as he will be. We fight a spiritual battle as soldiers for the Kingdom of God, which through our Lord and Saviour, Jesus Christ, the King of all kings and Lord of heaven's armies of angels, we already have the victory! Praise be to God! Jesus already won the battle over the enemy through His death and resurrection from the dead. It is He who teaches us how to fight, as supernatural warriors, with all spiritual authority through the power of His name.

God taught me that every interaction and experience that we have on this earth, whether good or bad, is of spiritual influence. Whether it be by the Holy Spirit, the human spirit, a ministering spirit (angel), or an evil spirit (demon), all life on earth is the physical experience of a spiritual nature. That is why a relationship with God is one of the spirit. All that we see in the physical is influenced by the spiritual. There is a vast spiritual realm, beyond the natural eye, that is greater than that of the physical, and only by God's grace can we navigate through it successfully. This happens only when our spirit man is developed and prepared by the Spirit of God to do so. Remember that the Spirit of God lives inside of us, and as spiritual beings, we are eternal in our existence. Therefore, our lifestyles must be one of the spirit, the Holy Spirit. The life on this earth is but fleeting. The life that remains is eternal. We must be able to come to the point where we overcome obstacles and challenges in the physical realm because we know its spiritual origin, and declare our Kingdom authority in Jesus' mighty name (Ephesians 6:12). In living a lifestyle of worship, we will frequently encounter opposition, trials and numerous temptations, but the battle is the Lord's. He will fight for us. When we repent of our sins, become clothed in His armour of light, and are covered by His blood, there is nothing that we cannot overcome. And praise is critical in the arsenal of our warfare.

Praise brings forth victory over the enemy, because praise ignites the fire of the Holy Spirit within us. God is an all-consuming fire and will incinerate any works of darkness in His path (Leviticus 9:24; 10:1, Hebrews 12:29). If you can use your imagination, the Holy Spirit is much like a fire inside of us, like a well-oiled lamp, waiting to be conflagrated into a ball of powerful flame. When we praise the Lord continuously, that fire grows from a spark into a well-lit flame, which grows bigger and bigger the more that we praise. This is a spiritual occurrence. Praise is therefore a mighty weapon. The enemy cannot bear to be in the presence of praises unto the Lord Jesus Christ. It paralyses his works and he has to flee. Praise ascends like a spiral of flames and erupts through the second heaven like a volcano. The enemy cannot come near to it. His works are destroyed, his plans are crushed and he himself is defeated. When we praise the Lord Jesus, the enemy can speak no lies into our ears, nor plant seeds of wickedness into our hearts. We become completely available for the Lord's use, as we begin to recognise who He is in us, who we are in Him, and how with Him and through Him, nothing is impossible.

The second book of Chronicles in the Bible, gives an epic example of the strategy of praise and the resulting powerful victory over our enemies. Chapter 20:1-30 shows the explosive outcome that results when praise *to* God and faith *in* God are combined. This was the scenario: the enemies of Judah and Jerusalem were on their way to annihilate everyone in the kingdom and they were powerless to do anything about it. Judah and Jerusalem were vastly outnumbered and did not stand a chance. With his natural eyes and human emotions, King Jehoshaphat began to panic. He could have perceived the matter to be one where the approaching armies were fierce men acting on their own efforts, and so the solution could have been to send out his army to fight and to die as men, and to hide the women and children with the hope of survival. No. King Jehoshaphat knew the spiritual origin of this deadly opposition, and so he went to the only One who could deliver him and his people. He sought the Lord with prayerful petition as a humble servant, coupled with the fasting and prayers of his people, and the Lord heard their cries. Had they not been living lives which were righteous in God's eyes, the result may have been much different. But the Lord said these words in response: *"Do not be afraid nor dismayed because of this great multitude, for the battle is not yours, but God's… You will not need to fight in this battle. Position yourselves, stand still and see the salvation of the Lord, who is with you, O Judah and Jerusalem! Do not fear or be dismayed; tomorrow go out against them, for the Lord is with you*" (verses 15-17). What assurance we have that the God who created all things and has the power over every nation, fights for those who love Him. Jehoshaphat **became strengthened by the word of God**, and his reaction to God's word was not doubt or fear, but praise. He, his priests and all of his people began to worship and sing praises unto the Lord. **They exalted His name over their situation.** Early the next morning the King of Judah sent forth his army who were led not by archers or extravagantly armoured horse-men, but by worshippers. What faith and obedience it took, for **worshippers** to **lead the army of God's people.** The priests led the men of war singing "*Praise the Lord; for His mercy endures forever*", and God began to fight! Did He fight in the physical? Of course not, because God is Spirit. Yet because He is God, He destroyed every evil assignment of Satan against His children in the spirit, in the midst of their praises, and so the battle manifested in the natural. Need-less to say, all of Judah's enemies were massacred by their own blades, and King Jehoshaphat and his people were able to rejoice over their defeated enemies and carry back three days' worth of spoils to the people at home. Can we not apply every aspect of this account to our own lives? How much more will the Lord fight for us when we call upon the name of Jesus? Can we not also witness the power of God and victory over our enemies when we operate with praise, faith and obedience? Most assuredly so.

Praise lifts up the name of Jesus, and there is power in His name to destroy all manner of evil imaginable. The Lord spoke to me about His name. This is what He said:

"My name is Jesus – the salvation of all mankind. The anointed ruler of all, your salvation. The Saviour of all. Jesus. (Pause) *Jesus. The name above every other name. My name is key to overcoming your enemy; to jumping over every hurdle; to overcoming every obstacle. Speak the name of the Lord, your God – Jesus! For at the sound of My name, evil takes notice. They take notice of the vessel through which My name comes. They know when the breath behind the speaking of My name contains the power of My Spirit, and they <u>must</u> bow. My name is the greatest above every other name. Reverence it, for it is holy and powerful. Be aware of the power with which you speak My name, for My Great Spirit is upon you and lives within you."*
(For scriptural reference, read Matthew 1:21, Luke 10:17).

We have the power of the voice to speak the name of Jesus boldly, with all authority, knowingly and confidently, being assured that evil *must* bow, evil *must* flee and that the enemy *must* scamper. We need to remember the power that our Lord's name holds. It is no mere word; it symbolizes the greatness and conquering power of the God of justice and truth (Isaiah 9:6). We must also remember to use it wisely, knowing that we shall be held accountable for its use (Exodus 20:7; Matthew 12:36,37).

PRAISE BRINGS PURPOSE. PRAISE BRINGS POWER.

The perfect will of God is free to take precedence in our lives when we commit to praising Him continuously. There is a direct alignment with the perfect will of God that occurs in the midst of our praise, and Satan is powerless to do anything about it. We become aligned with the Holy Spirit, and His desires for us become our desires for our own lives. His plans become our daily assignments, that we may grow in spiritual wisdom and understanding of who He is, who He is in us, who we are in Him, what He wants to happen and what He wants us to do, when we ought to do it and who to do it with. His answers to our prayers are manifested in their perfect timing as we operate victoriously over obstacles and hindrances, in our authority to rebuke their source of origin.

As believers in Jesus Christ our three main weapons against the enemy are praise, prayer and the Word of God. Each on its own is tremendously effective and absolutely necessary in our spiritual walk. Necessary not only as representatives of Christ, but also as citizens of God's Kingdom on the earth, that His Kingdom will be established in our lives and in the lives of those on whom we have an influence. His principles, His policies and His ordinances must be carried out, as flesh is removed in us and through synchronisation with the Holy Spirit, we allow Him to have His way in us. Through praise, God's Kingdom becomes established on the earth as His Lordship is declared, and so wherever we go in His name, there will His Kingdom be also. Praise, coupled with obedience, therefore allows us to be Kingdom planters on the earth.

On its own, praise is more effective than prayer because the enemy cannot steal it or oppose it. When done out of a pure heart, how can we ever praise the Lord Jesus amiss? However, when praise comes forth, it clears the way for our prayers to ascend to the Lord without hindrance (Psalm

141:2, Revelation 8:4). Prayer in itself ascends like thick smoke into the heavens, but coupled with the fire of praise, and the fiercely piercing sword of the Spirit (the Word of God), they form a spiritual juggernaut that the enemy is completely helpless against. God's holy angels can easily come to our aid as He sends them with answers to our prayers. And as we pray, and dare I say, praise without ceasing, we precisely align ourselves with the movement of His Spirit as our answered prayers become manifested before our eyes, in His timing. Praise therefore births God's purpose in our lives.

What then is the power of God? Can the earth contain it? Can our minds truly conceive the totality of the power of the Almighty, all-powerful, invincible God? Not in this lifetime. But contrary to what you may have thought before, God's power is not a finite source or physical force. **The power of God is His unmatched authority and capability to do all things, simply because He alone is God.** He has the greatest and final authority. He *can* because He *is*. He can do the impossible and there is nothing that He cannot do. But that we may *know* that He is God, the Lord God demonstrates His power through manifest signs and wonders, beyond the natural capability or explanation of man, seen as miracles before our eyes. These can be shown in the form of divinely supernatural healing, revelation of things that we could never know, opened doors of opportunity, surprises and instantaneous successes, divine alignment and unmerited favour in the eyes of men. There is deliverance from the grasp of Satan as he holds some in the tightly squeezing grip of drug addiction, pornography, homosexuality, idolatry, financial lack and poverty, shame, guilt and fear. It is the manifestation of the impossible before our eyes, where the invisible becomes seen and the unnatural becomes an anomaly — that is the manifest power of God in our lives. It is the ability to walk as a spiritual being of supernatural prowess, drawing on the source of such power, from a spiritual plane to a physical plane — that is when we *walk* in God's power. Like Peter and Stephen (Acts 5:15,16; 6:8) to name only two, when we declare a word and see it come to pass, even to the works of creation that then submit in obedience — that is the power of the Holy Spirit working in us. Those who have eyes to see in the spirit realm will see and know the source of such power, that all may know that the Lord Jesus, He is God.

Praise sets the foundation for God's power to be manifested in our lives. The lifestyle of worship must therefore be one where the impossible is possible through the power of the name of Jesus. It takes faith, it takes obedience and it begins with praise. We cannot expect to see the power of God at work in our lives, nor walk in it, nor operate in it if we do not send forth praises which exalt the name of the source of all power and might Himself, Jesus Christ. May we therefore endeavour in all things to praise the Lord, for surely He *is* good, and indeed, His mercy endures forevermore.

Chapter 5

LEARNING TO HEAR GOD'S VOICE

Chapter 5

LEARNING TO HEAR GOD'S VOICE

Do you remember the analogy of the sheep and the Shepherd in Chapter 1? The Lord taught us that when we belong to Him, we will hear His voice, that we may follow Him (John 10:3-5). But in a world where so many voices seek to imitate God's voice of righteousness, how can we be sure that we are really hearing from Him? It can be confusing, and often misleading when we are uncertain of whose voice we are hearing. Is it God or our own thoughts? To know our God, we must spend time with Him. And that is the key to hearing His voice – time in His presence through prayer, worship, reading His Word and waiting upon Him.

A PERSONAL RELATIONSHIP

Worship leads to the development of a personal relationship with God. A faithful lifestyle of worship causes us to become God's friends (James 2:23). How do you become friends with someone? Don't you take the time to get to know the person? You make the effort to get to know who they are, where they live, what they do, the things that they like and dislike, their personality, character and temperament, and how they feel about you in return. You learn to trust them with secrets and can depend on them to be there for you when you need them. You pass through good times and hard times, celebrations and sorrows. With each passing day you spend with this person, your friendship becomes stronger and stronger. How much more so with the Lord? Can you say that you are a friend of God? Can He trust you with His secrets? (Psalm 25:14). Do you know Him that well, and do you answer Him when He calls? Do you do what He asks because you love Him? Do you even spend time with Him? Since the beginning, in the Garden of Eden, we see that God's original intention was that He may fellowship with us. God loved to meet with Adam every evening and talk with Him (Genesis 3:8).

Somehow the stringencies of religion have separated mankind from personally knowing our Creator to instead being content at merely acknowledging His existence. Before we come into the knowledge of who God truly is, we tend to think of Him as a great, wondrous, unreachable God, whose glory we are unworthy to behold. Not so at all. The blood of Jesus made it possible for us to boldly come before the Lord in His holiness, as we are cleansed from sin and reconciled to Him (Hebrews 9:12-28; 4:16). Because of Jesus' sacrifice, God's original intention for a personal relationship with Him has been restored to us, where we know without a doubt that He is indeed reachable. In fact, He is right here with us; as soon as we should call upon His name, by His Holy Spirit, He is here (Matthew 18:20). It is with this knowledge that we are free to draw nearer to God and He promises to draw nearer to us in return (James 4:8). This pleases God, when through our own thoughts and perceptions, we no longer view ourselves as strangers to Him, but as His very own beloved children longing earnestly to befriend our Father. We begin that relationship with a conversation.

HELLO FATHER

Speech is free-flowing and unhindered when the mind is at rest. When the thoughts of the flesh lay silent and the mind no longer is burdened with the cares of the physical life - that is when the soul is opened to flow upwards to the presence of a holy God. What would you say to your Father should you behold Him before you? What words would come out of your mouth? Those are the words you want your Father to hear. **That is the art of prayer.**

Prayer is essential to living a lifestyle of worship. When He was on the earth, the Lord Jesus needed to be in constant communication with the Father in heaven. How much more so do we? Jesus was a master of the art of prayer: He separated himself from the distractions of the world around Him and went into a secret place with the Father, where He could pour out His heart to Him and hear from heaven in return. He often subdued His flesh through fasting, so that His spirit could arise to tap into spiritual things, being led by the Holy Spirit who was upon Him. He was disciplined and diligent to pray without ceasing and to remain constantly plugged in to the source of His strength. He prayed whether

He felt like it or not, because He knew that He could not complete His assignment on earth without the manifest presence of God to empower Him. That is what we too must do, so that we may:

1. Have effective communication with God, knowing His heart and mind about any matter that concerns us and the persons within our sphere of influence;
2. Be united with Him and synchronised with the movements of His Spirit in new times and seasons, so that we may know what to do and when to act, and;
3. Become empowered through the mercy of God and His grace that we may have the strength to endure any situation in life that we may be faced with.

The Lord gave us the basic model for communication with Him, beginning and ending with praise. He showed us this when He taught us how to pray. Let us briefly break down the "Our Father" taken from Matthew chapter 6 verses 9-13 (KJV):

9-*"Our Father which art in heaven, Hallowed be Thy name."* – Jesus teaches us to acknowledge the Father in heaven and to make is name holy. His name is set apart from every other and is to be revered. He alone is God. That is how our prayers should begin.

10 – *"Thy kingdom come. Thy will be done, in earth as it is in heaven."* – Jesus teaches us that where the name of the Lord is exalted, His Kingdom is established. Therefore heavenly principles and policies apply and all things act in submission to His Kingship. We surrender our own will to God, by the humble yielding of self. It is then that *His* perfect will, desires, plans, purposes, decrees and ordinances are released in heaven and are manifested on the earth as He wills it to be. God releases the word from His throne and it is carried out by His angels from the heavenly realm into the earthly one.

11-13 -*"Give us this day our daily bread. And forgive us our debts, as we forgive our debtors. And lead us not into temptation, but deliver us from evil"* – Jesus shows that after God is revered and we submit to His Lordship, we can then make our petition before Him. As we saw in Chapter 4, praise clears the way for our prayers to come forth. He taught us to ask, and it shall be given unto us, and not to do so selfishly, but with all sincerity of heart (Matthew 7:7, James 4:3).

Therefore as He gave us the perfect example, we can ask our Father for daily provision, for mercy and forgive-ness for our sins (knowing that we will receive it only when we forgive others), for deliverance from the works of the devil and from demonic activity, including divine protection, and for strength to overcome temptation that we may not sin.

13 (end) – *"For Thine is the kingdom and the power and the glory forever. Amen"* – The Lord taught us that when we have made our petition before the throne of grace, we are to have faith that our God will grant unto us what we have asked. Therefore we ought to praise Him, because He is God, all powerful and mighty throughout all of eternity.

Prayer is therefore the medium that we can use to get to the Father, through our Lord Jesus Christ. As His Word says, *"For there is one God, and one mediator between God and men – the man Christ Jesus"* (1 Timothy 2:5), and no one else. He said that anything we ask in His name, He will do it (John 14:13,14), and may we remember also, in *His* timing, not ours. We are able to pray with our own words, prayers of petition (asking for things), lamentation (grief/sorrow), surrender, repentance, prophetic declaration (authorit-atively speaking the unseen into existence, as He reveals to us) and intercession (on behalf of another) and whatever the Spirit leads us to pray. The point is that we can carry our concerns to our God because He cares for us, knowing that He hears us and that He will show up (1 Peter 5:7). In Psalm 91:14-16, the Lord says, *"Because he has set his love upon Me, therefore I will deliver him; I will set him on high, because he has known My name. He shall call upon Me, and **I will answer him**; I will be with him in trouble; I will deliver him and honour him. With long life I will satisfy him, and show him My salvation"* (Emphasis added). What a beautiful promise of safety, deliverance, protection and salvation from our God. We are never alone, and it is this constant communication with our God that reminds us of His continuous presence and abiding love.

Prayer also enables us to wage war against the enemy *and win*. It has great power beyond the limitations of natural hindrances and boundaries, to destroy great boulders and to bring forth the spirit into the natural. In prayer we speak forth a matter and see it come to be. We have what we say in the name of Jesus Christ. Our words are powerful and effect change when spoken in alignment with God's will. When we speak life, life is. We can bind demons, loose blessings and lay hold to what rightfully belongs to us which the devil has stolen (Matthew 12:29). We must pray in faith, believing and not doubting the rivers that prayer can dry up or the barricades that it can break down, and the lives that it can cause to be turned around. This is because we war not against flesh and blood but against the unseen in the spirit realm, and our weapons are therefore not physical ones but Godly spiritual ones (Ephesians 6:12; 2 Corinthians 10:4). Our Lord Jesus already gave us the authority over all the power of the devil (Luke 10:19) and so in prayer we must stand in that authority as the children of God. No weapon formed against us can prosper. None. And if God be for us, then who can be against us? We have the privilege of fighting a war that has already been won by Jesus Christ, our Lord. In prayer we must therefore gird ourselves with the armour of the Spirit of God (Ephesians 6:14-17; Isaiah 59:17), as soldiers in His army, and pray without ceasing.

Never stop praying. How would you survive if you stopped drinking water? With every passing day, your body would get weaker and weaker, your organs would begin to shut down, your blood circulation would practically grind to a halt and you would die from the effects of dehydration. Don't dehydrate your spirit. Prayer connects us to the river of living waters, Jesus Christ Himself, and His waters contain eternal sustenance and the life-giving power of God. Every day that we go without prayer, our spirit gets weaker, our armour falls off and we become live prey to the wiles of the devil. Of course, living unrighteously or outside of the will of God causes our own self-defeat, as the enemy would have a legal right to intervene in our daily lives. The Bible says that *"The effective, fervent prayer of a **righteous** man avails much"* (James 5:16, Emphasis added), and that *"the face of the Lord is against them that do evil"* (Psalm 34:16). A righteous man is a man who lives in obedience to God. Therefore we cannot expect our prayers, however fervent, however eloquent, and however powerfully clad to pack much of a punch into the spirit realm, when our armour is covered with the mud of sin instead of the blood of Jesus Christ.

When we pray, we ought to let the Holy Spirit lead us. Ask the Lord what to pray and to lead you in the right direction. Only He knows what is happening in the unseen realm. If you possess the gift of tongues, let your spirit pray and the Holy Spirit will begin to pray through you. He knows our weaknesses and makes intercession for us with even unspeakable groanings (Romans 8:26). If this may be new to you, I would suggest beginning by praying in tongues for an hour straight for a few days to really stir up the gift, so that you begin to truly be led by the Spirit. This practice will surely help to increase your sensitivity to Him in prayer. He often gives us an image or a name of a familiar individual, ideas and concepts, situations and circumstances that require our attention. That is when prayer truly becomes life-changing because we are no longer praying our own will (in the flesh), but God's will (in the Spirit).

MEAN WHAT YOU SAY

Too often our prayers and our songs of worship are filled with empty repetitions. How would you feel if every time someone spoke to you they always said the same things? Wouldn't that become monotonous and boring? Not to mention if they didn't even mean their own words. Not anymore. God is a person, with feelings and emotions just like we have. He created us not only to look like Him, in His image, but also to resemble Him in our being (Genesis 1:26). That means that He laughs, feels grief, gets angry, feels remorse and feels joy, just like we do. He created *us* that way, so that we may relate to *Him*. Why then do we give Him meaningless words? On their own, words mean nothing. They only have meaning when it is the speaker's conscious intention to relay a message. I once asked the

Lord if He ever gets tired of hearing the same worship songs over and over again. He said no. What He listens for are the hearts of men. When we mean the words that we say or sing to Him with all sincerity, it comes from inside of our hearts. God's Kingdom reigns inside of our hearts. Faith and belief in the words that we give to Him establishes the connection between our earthly existence and the heavenly realm rooted inside of us by the Spirit of God, and that is what ushers in the anointing. It is a Kingdom connection from our spirit to His Spirit that pleases Him and provides an open invitation for Him to come into our place of worship, wherever we are. Have you ever noticed in a meeting or service, for instance, when you sing songs unto God or repeat prayers that you are familiar with off of the top of your head, nothing happens? There is no anointing, no movement of the Spirit? That is because you are not connected to Him. However, notice when you mean the words that you sing, or the prayers that you speak, you begin to feel His presence. You feel warmth when His Spirit is near, you may cry, pores become raised and you may become filled with joy or peace that you did not have before. People may receive healing and deliverance, you may fall to your knees, smell His sweet fragrance, worship in tongues and in that meeting, nothing goes according to plan, yet everything falls together perfectly nonetheless. That is the power of the anointing of God. And that is when you begin to hear His voice.

THE VOICE

So far, we have talked about a one-way communication with God, but we do know that for communication to truly be effective, it must be two-way. Not only are we to speak to God, but we must hear what He has to say in return. Often times, it is He who initiates the conversation. God speaks. In fact, He is always speaking to us. We unfortunately just do not listen for His voice.

> *"The voice of the Lord is over the waters; the God of glory thunders; the Lord is over many waters. The voice of the Lord is powerful; the voice of the Lord is full of majesty. The voice of the Lord breaks the cedars, yes, the Lord splinters the cedars of Lebanon. He makes them also skip like a calf, Lebanon and Sirion like a young wild ox. The voice of the Lord divides the flames of fire. The voice of the Lord shakes the wilderness; the Lord shakes the Wilderness of Kadesh. The voice of the Lord makes the deer give birth, and strips the forests bare;"* – Psalm 29: 3-9.

This Psalm speaks not only of the power and majesty of God's audible voice from His throne in heaven, but the impact that it has on creation when He speaks, from the spirit into the natural. God rarely speaks in a physically audible manner nowadays, because He does not need to. We have the Holy Spirit who is the person of God and it is He who speaks to us while we are yet on this earth. There are many different ways to hear His voice. What I will share are what I have experienced, and they are:

1. In His written Word (*logos,* in the Greek), the Bible;
2. In His spoken word (*rhema,* in the Greek) and;
3. Through dreams and visions.

The one common entity in every possible facet of God's voice is the Holy Spirit. Without Him, we would hear nothing, and be in complete darkness without the light of the Word to guide our footsteps. That is why after we have received the Lord Jesus as Saviour and the Holy Spirit comes and lives inside of us, we automatically begin to hear His voice and to know who He is. Be wary to trust the counsel of anyone who does not have the Holy Spirit within them, who says that they have heard from God, unless you receive confirmation from another person who does have God's Spirit within them.

WORD!

Jesus is the Word (John 1:1; 1:14), and from the first letter to the last full stop, the entire Bible is *all about Him*. He is the Author of it and His Spirit led the pen of every man that wrote in it (2 Timothy 3:16). The Scriptures were relevant when they were written, they were relevant when they were assembled into what we know as the Christian Bible, and they are relevant up to this day, because God is still God, then and now and forever. As long as He exists, His Word still stands (Matthew 24:35). His Word is never to be taken merely at face value, for He often has a deeper meaning in what He is saying. It is written as line, upon line, upon line, and precept, upon precept, upon precept (Isaiah 28:10), to be understood at greater depths with divine wisdom and understanding. For us to receive any revelation of the meaning of the Scriptures that we may hear God's voice, they must be read prayerfully, asking the Holy Spirit to reveal to us what the Lord is saying through His Word.

The Word of God is a rudder to the rudderless ship along the stormiest of waves, and the compass to the vessel that has been spun in any direction. It is there to guide us in every experience throughout this earthly life, that we may lay hold unto salvation; be corrected; be encouraged and strengthened; and that He may reveal His nature to us. We can never truly understand God's nature without the Holy Spirit. That is why our Lord Jesus Christ sent Him to us as our Comforter and Helper, and He teaches us everything that we need to know (1 John 2:27; John 14:26).

When we know the Word of God, we can be led by His Spirit as students by a good teacher. That way, our lives will bear the good fruit of righteousness and we will avoid the deception and lies of false teachings and philosophies, and any other means that Satan may use to lead us away from the truth. Jesus is the truth. His Word is truth. As it says in Psalm 19:7-11, His Word is perfect (complete and lacking nothing), sure, right, pure, clean, true and righteous. Knowing it is the greatest treasure, more than any amount of fine gold, and in obeying it, there is great reward. God said that we should study to show ourselves approved to Him (2 Timothy 2:15). What greater reward is there in knowing, believing and living by His Word? God taught me this:

"Can a sword fight on its own, or does a man not wield it? Can an unskilled fighter win his combat, though His sword be brilliant? No, daughter. He shall perish, and his sword remain to be taken into spoils and wielded by another. And so you must be a skilled warrior, both in My Word and in deed. You must be able to wield My sword, for it is a heavy one to manipulate, and the enemy is more skilled than you know." (For scriptural reference, read Ephesians 6: 17, Hebrews 4:12).

Can a soldier know what to do if he cannot hear the voice of his commander? Not only is God's Word the sword of the Spirit, it is His voice that speaks to our spirit through the revelation by His Spirit. Therefore, in living a lifestyle of worship, we must know the voice of the One whom we call Father and Lord. Time invested in reading His Word is absolutely essential for our growth of spirit, and evolvement of skill as His chosen swordsmen.

A STILL SMALL VOICE

"Then He said, 'Go out, and stand on the mountain before the Lord.' And behold, the Lord passed by, and a great and strong wind tore into the mountains and broke the rocks in pieces before the Lord, but the Lord was not in the wind; and after the wind an earthquake, but the Lord was not in

the earthquake; and after the earthquake a fire, but the Lord was not in the fire; and **after the fire a still small voice***. So it was, when Elijah heard it, that he wrapped his face in his mantle and went out and stood in the entrance of the cave. Suddenly a voice came to him, and said, 'What are you doing here, Elijah?'"* (1 Kings 19:11-13. Emphasis added).

The Lord God showed His prophet Elijah, that although He is the Almighty, all-powerful God, He speaks to us by His Spirit. We are not to seek God in great signs and wonders such as winds and earthquakes and fires, for although He commands nature and all of creation, His voice is not in such things. To be clear, signs and wonders are a tremendous display of God's glory and power, and even His love, but *not* His voice. What is a voice? *Is it not the vocal expression of the breath of a man?* Is God's breath not His Spirit? In the original Hebrew language that most of the Old Testament is written in, the word used for "breath" is synonymous with the word used for "spirit", which is *"ruach"*. The Spirit of God is the only impression of God's voice that we can personally receive in the earthly plane, and not outward signs that our natural eyes can behold. This is not to limit God's capability, for indeed He can do all things, but remember that God is Spirit. If it is that His Spirit lives inside of us, then when He speaks to us it is our *spiritual* ears that hear a sound, which is then interpreted by our minds and we react in the body. Signs and wonders appeal *not* to the spiritual ears, but to the natural eyes that we may see them in the flesh. When God speaks to us personally, this communication is internally expressed and outwardly manifested, and not the other way around.

Physical signs and wonders may *represent* God and may be a form of communication to us that is not speech, but instead have meanings pertaining to direction, times and seasons, confirmation of spiritual inclinations, warnings and memorials. He may use such things to reveal a matter or to teach us something by way of visible demonstration. We represent God on the earth, but we are not His voice (Isaiah 8:18). Yet He may use us to demonstrate His power and love in the life of another. A teacher who hands out coloured building blocks to demonstrate the concept of team work has not actually spoken until he opens his mouth and the students hear his explanation. Until he speaks, the students may perceive the blocks to have varying uses depending upon their individual levels of understanding, leading some of them off track. It is the voice that brings clarity. That is the Holy Spirit. When He speaks to us, it is no mere concept or display that is subject to critique. It is an inner voice that guides us, that we may know His heart and mind concerning a matter. For the avoidance of all doubt, know that when God is speaking to you, your spirit will stir within you. This is because when He speaks, the body does not react independently, and neither does the soul. Can you hear God with your own thoughts or imaginations? Can you force yourself to hear? If He has not spoken, then there is nothing to hear. When God speaks, your spirit knows, for it is His Spirit who is inside of you, who resonates from within. Two things worthy of remembering when you believe that God is speaking to you are:

1. He always sticks to the Scriptures. He points you back to His *logos* Word, and it is this guidance that keeps us from falling into deception. That is another reason why it is important for us to know the Scriptures.
2. He usually repeats Himself. He may tell you the same thing in various ways over a period of time, and confirm it through other people who you may come into contact with, and even by having you experience "co-incidences" that are not just by chance.

We ought not to seek after signs and wonders themselves, but after the truth, so that in seeking the truth, signs and wonders can confirm it. Many are deceived by the demonic signs and wonders that exist (Exodus 7:22), such as stigmata, levitation, bleeding and crying statues, apparitions appearing as Mary, religious saints and as people known to you, and false miracles performed by wolves in sheep's clothing. As I said in Chapter 3, you shall know them by their fruit. If the fruit produced by supposed men and women of God are not in alignment with the truth of God's Word, then surely any signs or wonders that they perform are not from God. Such things are used by Satan to draw our attention away from Jesus Christ and towards the glory of a human being and ultimately to himself. Remember the words of our Lord Jesus when He said, *"For false christs and false prophets will appear and perform great signs and miracles to deceive, if possible, even the elect"* (Matthew 24:24). His Word also says in 2 Thessalonians 2:9 that, *"The coming of the lawless one is according to the working of Satan, with all power, signs, and lying wonders"*. On their own, signs and wonders may lead to deception, if they are not accompanied by the voice of God, that is, revelation by His Holy Spirit. Let us therefore not seek after such things. For although the Lord will use them as He sees fit to demonstrate or to communicate a matter for us to physically observe, it pleases Him more that we have faith in Him and that we seek Him in the spirit. *"Because you have seen Me, you have believed. Blessed are those who have not seen and yet have believed"* (John 20:29).

The Lord said this to me:

*"I have spoken and it shall be. It shall be as I have decreed. Daughter, let not your eyes wander. Let them not look away from Me, nor be distracted by any other shining light. I am the light of the world. Any other light is but a farce, for such is purposed to lead you into darkness. A false light that brings much despair. Let not your eyes be darkened by any false light. My light is pure and unmatched, for **in My light is My voice.** And it is so that You shall know Me. Listen for My voice. If you do not hear Me, then I am not in that light, and that is but a snare. Be not attracted to strange lights, My daughter, for they shall shine from many directions. They shall seek to pull you into many strange directions and cause you confusion. Listen for My voice. Then you shall know whether it is I, the Lord your God, or another."* (For scriptural reference, read John 8:12, Ezekiel 1:28; 43:2, Acts 22:6-9).

Jesus is the light. He lives in us by His Spirit, therefore His light is in us (2 Corinthians 4:6,7; Proverbs 20:27). He commanded us to let *this* light shine brightly before the eyes of men, that they may see our good *works* and glorify the Father in heaven (Matthew 5:16). As I explained the relationship between the spirit, the soul and the body in Chapter 2, *the light of God, His Spirit in us*, shines forth from our spirit and is seen in the things that we say and do. That is how we let our light shine. In God's light is His voice. When we see His light, we hear His voice. The light that we shine is not His voice, but within in it lies His voice, as we are led by His Spirit. Therefore the things that we say and do in His name ought to come from His Spirit, as we are led by the Spirit and not after the works of the flesh. When He speaks, we hear Him and we carry out what He leads us to do. When what we say and do in the body is aligned with God's Word, it is a testament of His voice before the eyes of others. That is why we must be able to discern when the light that we see before us is a strange one, or a dark, cold, false one, if it does not align with God's Word. We see that all of life is connected by the Spirit of God, in His *logos* Word and His *rhema* word, and in the actions of mankind. We must desire the gift of discernment of spirits, so that we may be able to hear God's voice clearly, in the inner man, and in what we see before us, to know whether or not it is Him speaking.

We can practise hearing God's voice by a discipline called journaling. Similar to taking record of an event or conversation, journaling allows us to record our conversation with the Lord. Following (and even during) prayer, with settled thoughts and minimal distractions, the Holy Spirit begins to speak to us. According to how you are led by Him, you should write down what He is saying as He is saying it. Journaling can also take the form of question and answer, or just asking Him to speak whatever may be on His heart. Then, begin to write His response. Relax your conscious thoughts and allow the Spirit to lead you. You will find that what you have written is beyond your own thoughts or ways. The Lord will take you from a place of knowledge, to a place of wisdom and great understanding. *By no means is this automatic writing*, which is demonic in nature. Instead, journaling is taking record of your communication with God, and with practice, you begin to hear more clearly, and more accurately. So get a notebook, and begin to write what the Spirit of the Lord is saying to you.

WHAT DO YOU SEE?

The Lord also speaks to us in dreams and visions, awakening the senses of our spiritual eyes. Not only will He speak to us by internal impression, but He also shows us images when we are awake and asleep for a specific purpose. Now, the seer realm is tremendously prophetic in nature, and to encompass it all is beyond the scope of this chapter and book, but what I will mention briefly is the "how". How is it that we are able to receive messages from God in the form of a snapshot image or rolling film when we are awake, or as a clear dream when we are asleep? By the Holy Spirit. He can reveal to us spiritual matters of the unseen realm, plans of the enemy and the plans of God. He can show us past and future events and reveal mysteries that no one else can ever know. He can warn us, correct us, instruct us, reveal subconscious feelings to us and even appear to us. This is so that we may act in the physical through prayer, behavioural modifications and the carrying out of specific tasks in our daily lives. This is not new, and dreams and visions have been recorded numerous times throughout Scripture, affecting the lives of characters like Jacob (Genesis 28:12), Joseph (Genesis 37:5), Daniel (Chapters 7-10), Ezekiel (Chapter 1 and more), Peter, Stephen, Paul (Acts) and John

(Revelation) to name only a few. The point is that when we receive a dream or a vision from the Holy Spirit, we must act on it. One important thing that we can do is to journal it in detail, even taking note of the date and time it was received. We must ask the Holy Spirit to reveal to us its meaning, and follow through with effective prayer. When the Lord speaks to us in a dream or a vision, it is because He wants to draw our attention to something that is important in our lives and even the lives of others. So never ignore a vision or dream from God. Seek the counsel of the Holy Spirit, and do your part accordingly.

GET THE MESSAGE

We know that there are various ways that we can communicate with each other indirectly, utilizing the assistance of others. God does this through His holy angels. God can communicate with us outside of the Holy Spirit, that is, we can receive a message from His ministering spirits, carrying out their assignment to assist us (Hebrews 1:14). God's angels represent Him as His messengers, but they are not His voice. They relay a message and communicate with us as spiritual beings according to God's will. Imagine that you are the Prime Minister of your country, and you send a member of parliament to represent you at a meeting, where they deliver a verbal address on your behalf. When they speak, is it your voice that the people hear, or is it your message? Exactly – it is your message. So it is with the Lord and His angels. When the Lord speaks from the throne room in heaven, His angels carry out His instructions. They do nothing of their own will or accord, and every interaction with humankind is on assignment from God. We are not to pray to them, or worship them in any manner (Colossians 2:18; Revelation 19:10), but to receive their assistance and their message with humility and thanksgiving to our God. Some people have had the privilege of seeing and interacting with angels in person, like Joshua and Mary did (Joshua 5:13-15; Luke 1:26-38), while others have seen them in dreams and visions like Ezekiel and Joseph did (Ezekiel 1:5-14; Matthew 1:20). The majority of people who have received angelic messages and assistance have not been able to see them, but have felt their heavenly presence. The gift of discernment of spirits once again, is essential to us knowing the nature of any spiritual presence in our midst and only the Holy Spirit can reveal this to us.

Another way that God may choose to send a message to us, is through the voice of His prophets. Prophets are anointed servants of God who speak His heart and mind (Amos 3:7). They are able to foretell a matter and speak a matter into existence by forth-telling it, being led only by the Spirit of God. Prophets have the authority by God to build up, encourage and comfort, as well as warn, give direction, pronounce judgement, pronounce (*not predict*) future events, and release spiritual gifts and offices of five-fold ministry. When a prophet speaks a word into one's life, it must be done in love and never to embarrass or humiliate the hearer. Deeply personal details are not to be revealed at all, much less publicly, and no matter what, it is never for material gain. We are able to determine whether or not a prophet is a false one, if their words released do not come to pass (Deuteronomy 18:22). When God gives a message, it shall come to pass because His Word cannot be returned to Him void (Isaiah 55:11). Prophecies release God's will into our lives and the acceptance of a prophetic word helps to shape our destiny in Christ. They usually seek to confirm that which has already been spoken to us by the Holy Spirit, and set us on a path to the fulfilling of our purpose on the earth. There is much more that can be said about the office of the prophet, the gift of prophecy and the spirit of prophecy (Revelation 19:10), and the roles that each plays in the Body of Christ. However, the point here is that we ought to be able to receive a message from God from the mouth of another human being, identifying the source of the message as the Spirit of God.

Therefore let us invest our time significantly in the presence of the Lord. Become disciplined in making the time every day to read the Scriptures and meditate on them, pray, worship, and wait to hear what the Lord will say to you. There is no short cut with God. If we truly desire to know Him, as our Father and our Friend, then we must get to know the Holy Spirit, who will teach us everything about our heavenly Father and our Lord and Saviour Jesus Christ.

Chapter 6

FEAR AND FAITH CANNOT MIX

Chapter 6

FEAR AND FAITH CANNOT MIX

DO NOT BE AFRAID

Throughout the Bible God tells us that we are not to be afraid 365 times. He insists on it, He repeats it, He stresses on it: *"Do not be afraid"*. Every time He appoints someone to do something, He says, *"Do not be afraid"*. Every time He is about to demonstrate His power and might, He says, *"Fear not"*. This may seem easy to do, in theory, but as believers in Jesus Christ, when we are faced with trials and troubles, it is not easy to be brave all of the time. Abraham, the patriarch of the nation of Israel, was called out from his homeland to leave all comfort, safety and familiarity behind, into a new place, never seen or heard of before. He feared.

Moses, the greatest leader of the children of Israel, was called to lead hundreds of thousands of slaves to freedom, while he was an eighty-year-old shepherd, and he was afraid. The greatest king of Israel, King David was persecuted and hunted like an animal by his predecessor King Saul, and by his very own son, Absalom. Many times, he feared for his life. On the night that He was arrested, Jesus our Lord, in preparing for His torture and gruesome death, cried tears of anguish and tremendous sorrow. He feared.

What made these men so great that their lives made such an impact on the history of mankind? It was their faith in God. They used faith in God to overcome their trials and to be victorious in accomplishing their assignments on the earth. Many times I have found myself afraid. This is what the Lord taught me:

"Child of the living God, you have nothing to fear, but fear itself. Do you understand that? **Fear is a crippling force used by demons to paralyze the sons of God, and keep them from reaching their full potential.** *Fear teaches you to believe in lies, and in what does not exist, out of the belly of the one who created lies. Fear belongs to the enemy. Therefore, you are not to fear. Do you see now, daughter, why I cannot accept the fearful believer? The believer who fears is controlled by Satan.*

Do not be under the control of any demon, daughter. Break free and denounce fear. Fear of life, fear of death, fear of harm and hurt, fear of sickness, fear of loneliness, fear of disease, fear of poverty. Rebuke all fear! Denounce it and destroy it in My great and powerful name. Declare peace, joy, prosperity, success, love, strength, courage, confidence, faith – the conqueror of fear, and truth. For so, I am the way, the truth and the life. Speak life into all things, and see Me do a great and marvellous work. I shall turn your fears into triumph, for all victory is Mine, and I am your redeemer. Trust also in Me, and daily behold the unfolding of My works." (For scriptural reference, read John 8:44; 14:6, Proverbs 18:21, Isaiah 41:10).

THROUGH THE CRACKS

Fear is a weapon of Satan against our minds. It is completely demonic in nature, whereby his evil spirits become attached to us when we open the doors of doubt and unbelief in the truth of the Word of God. They linger when we are at our moments of weakness, speaking lies and all manner of untruths into our ears, and should we listen and believe them, it is then that the spirit of fear takes hold (Job 4:14-21).

Our faith in God is like a shield against the devil. As long as our shield is up, he has no access to our personal lives. When we become anxious or worried concerning any matter in particular, the shield becomes weakened, and a crack forms in the shield. The enemy can than enter through that particular crack and manifest our fears into reality. That is why the things that we fear the most are usually what come to pass. Fear of illness clears the way for a spirit of infirmity to enter into our lives. Fear of poverty, the spirit of poverty. Fear of success or change, a spirit of oppression, causing stagnation and preventing advancement, and so it goes. This is what happened to Job in the Bible. As a devoted servant of God, Job had everything that a man could ever want: favour with God, a wife, children, good health, great wealth and influence. He loved his God and was committed to serving Him, yet, Job was fearful. He was afraid for his children. The enemy used Job's fears against him, and exactly what Job feared the most is what happened to him (Job 3:25). All of his children died, he lost all of his wealth and influence, he lost his health and he even lost the respect and support of his wife. It was not until Job surrendered to the perfect will of God, trusted Him and believed His promises that faith arose in him. God used Job's faith as a testament of His power over the enemy, as well as a demonstration of His mercy and grace. He restored to Job everything that He had lost, some twice more than he had before. How much more so with us?

FEAR IS POWER

When you believe that something negative exists, or in the possibility of an adverse event occurring, such a thing gains power over you. Your belief in the lie affects your ability to think clearly, your decision-making skills become dull, and your ability to distinguish between reality and truth becomes clouded - between how things appear, and what God says is His will. Fear then controls your life and keeps you from your destiny in Christ Jesus. Think of a bully. A bully is enticed by and feeds off of the fear of the weak-minded. When that bully knows that he is feared, he becomes addicted to that new power that he has to control, to manipulate and to force others to do what they do not want to do. He thrives off of it, and continually seeks more of it. So it is with the enemy. When he succeeds in causing you to doubt the greatness, power, mercy, love and truth that is God, our armour is let down and he moves in for the hit. He uses the spirit of fear to keep God's children in a state of mental paralysis and spiritual bondage that only faith in God can

FEAR AND FAITH CANNOT MIX

break. Don't you dare give the devil this kind of power over you.

When we are perpetually frightened, we limit the freedom of movement of the Spirit of God in our lives. God is telling you to open a business, but you are afraid to because you cannot see where the money will come from to do so, not knowing that He has an investor waiting around the corner to help you. Destiny averted. God is telling you to begin your ministry, but you are afraid to because you do not think that you are qualified enough. You listen to the enemy's lies in your mind that say, "No one will listen to you. You're too young/too old. You don't have enough money", not knowing God's plan to use you to demonstrate His love to others and to bring souls into His Kingdom. Purpose unfulfilled. Children fare well in the darkest of hours because they do not fear the unknown. Are we not called to be as children in the sight of our God? (Matthew 18:3). This too, applies to our faith in Him as our Father. Why let fear cripple your mind and trap you in a state of doubt and uncertainty? Why let fear keep you from doing what God says that you *can* do, because He is with you and will never leave you? Remember that a doubleminded man is unstable in all of his ways (James 1:8). When we are wavering on the rickety bridge of doubt, we will not receive anything from God until we can come to stand upon the Rock of stability, our Lord Jesus Christ. Is it really worth remaining in that place of bondage?

Fear only begets rejection and resentment of self, a plummeting of faith in who God is, and a decrease of self-worth. When you live a life that is controlled by fear, you forget your identity as a child of the King of Glory. You forget that you are loved beyond measure by the God who reigns as your King and your Father. Instead, you believe yourself to be unworthy to receive blessings, love and kindness, from God and man. You subject yourself to abuse, by both yourself and by others, at home, in the workplace, and even from the pulpit in the church. You forget that you have the all-powerful Spirit of the living God inside of you, and that you can call upon the God of heaven who will move the earth just to save you (Psalm 18:6-17). Do you see the heaviness and oppression that fear gives? How can we receive the promises of God if we do not believe that they exist? Can God use us to represent Him on the earth if we are not certain that He truly is our protector, provider, healer and deliverer? He cannot because we are bound by sin. It is not sinful to feel fear, for it surely is a common part of the experience of life, but indeed it *is* a sin to *be fearful* — to let fear keep you from believing God (Revelation 21:8). The Bible says that what is not of faith is sin, and we know that fear is the opposite of faith (Romans 14:23).

GOOD NEWS

The good news is that we have the power through our Saviour and Deliverer, Jesus Christ, to overcome the spirit of fear and to live out our time on the earth fulfilling our God-given purpose. Can you imagine what our lives would be like today if the Lord Jesus let the spirit of fear overtake Him, and keep Him from His destiny of being the Saviour of all mankind and the King over all creation? You and I would have zero hope for salvation, and hell-fire would instead be the fate of the entire world. Thank God that our Lord overcame His moments of fear by His unwavering faith and trust in God our Father. If this was the example that He set for us, then surely we can overcome fear as well.

The Lord Jesus taught me that we can do this by using the weapon of prayer. He taught me when in prayer to call out my fear by name, and renounce it, reject it and rebuke it in His name. He taught me to command the spirit of fear to loose its hold upon my life and denounce any power that it may have, by the power of the blood of the Lamb, in Jesus' mighty name. He reminded me of my authority over all the power of the enemy (Luke 10:19), and that I can decree and declare every manner of fear destroyed, in His name. That is what I would advise you to do also. Remember that we shall have what we say when we have faith that God will grant unto us the victory over our enemies (Mark 11:22-24). Therefore, cast out every fear by speaking the perfect love of God over your life (1 John 4:18). When we lean on God, seek Him first in all things and trust Him, He will most assuredly complete us. Therefore, replace the fear of success by declaring success and divine favour upon your endeavours (Ephesians 3:20). Replace the fear of lack by declaring supernatural prosperity and that the Lord shall supply all of your needs according to His riches in glory (Philippians 4:19). Replace the fear of illness or death by declaring that you shall *not* die, but live, and declare the works of the Lord (Psalm 118:17). Replace the fear of danger by declaring that no weapon of the enemy formed against you shall prosper (Isaiah 54:17) and that because the Lord is your refuge, no evil shall befall you (Psalm 91: 9,10). Getting the picture? Renounce every one of your fears by boldly and confidently speaking the Word of God over your life, out of your own lips. And last, but not least, replace your fear of the enemy by declaring your faith in God.

At all times, but *especially* in your moments of weakness, be conscious of what you are thinking about. If negative, accusing, demotivating, suspicious, presumptuous or otherwise discouraging thoughts begin to enter your mind, cut them off immediately – those are the lies of the devil. The moment you give ear to them, much less believe them, and God-forbid, repeat them out loud, you begin to shape your world into one of oppression and self-defeat. The Holy Spirit does not condemn, discourage or blame. He convicts, encourages and comforts. He does not lead you along a path of suspicion of others and doubt in God's ways. He enlightens your eyes to see the spiritual side of things, and strengthens your spirit that you may endure your trials. God has given us His Spirit of power, love and stability of thoughts and emotions (2 Timothy 1:7). Learning to recognise when the enemy is trying to weaken your shield with lies is absolutely necessary in overcoming every possible fear.

FAITH, THE FUEL

What then, is faith? According to Hebrews 11:1, *"faith is the substance of things hoped for, the evidence of things not seen"*, but do you really know what that means? Let us break it down. A substance is a form of physical matter. It exists in a state that can be transferred from one body to another, and can be contained within a vessel. Hope, is the positive belief that something good will happen. **Faith therefore, is the energy source that sustains positive belief.** You cannot believe if you do not have faith. Belief is the vehicle and faith is the fuel. Belief is the stove top and faith is the gas. The greater your faith, the stronger your belief. When you therefore believe God, you trust Him completely to act on your behalf. Without faith, it is absolutely impossible to please Him (Hebrews 6:11). When we come to God, we must believe that He is who He says that He is, and that He will do what He says that He will do. Like a father taking care of his son, if the boy does not believe that his father is his biological one, nor that his father will keep any of the promises that he made to him, how do you think that father would feel? He would surely be hurt and displeased, and leave whatever inheritance he had waiting for that son to another one who embraces him and trusts him. God is no different in that sense. Faith in who He is, and belief in His Word pleases Him greatly.

"Abraham believed God, and it was accounted to him for righteousness" (Galatians 3:6). Just as fearfulness is a sin in God's eyes, faith in Him makes us righteous. It makes us righteous not by anything that we can say or do, because our works alone cannot please Him, neither do we please Him by rigidly obeying His Word out of our own self-righteousness, but it is faith in God that causes us to believe Him and hence *obey* Him (Galatians 3:11). It is that trust and *obedience* which make us upright before Him. We can then be judged according to our integrity and uprightness because He delights in us (Psalm 18:20-24). Imagine this: the Lord God instructs you to speak a word of encouragement to a complete stranger. Although you may not know why, or what to say, because of your faith in Him, you *believe* that He has a purpose for doing so, and so you obey Him. He may instruct you to give an offering in church of a certain figure. Although you cannot see where you are going to get the money from to pay your bills, because of your faith in Him, you *believe* that He has a blessing in store for you, so you obey Him. The Lord may instruct you to leave

your family and friends and head off to another country to minister to the lost in that place. Although you have no clue how you are going to support yourself, or who you are going to meet, because of your faith in Him, you *believe* that He will supply you with all of the necessary resources and use you mightily for His Kingdom, and so you obey Him. Faith as you see, requires us to demonstrate our belief in God. When we do such a thing, we will surely be rewarded for our obedience to Him.

Faith in God aligns us with the promises of Abraham (Galatians 3:7), whereby we are counted amongst the children of Spiritual Israel (see Chapter 1), to receive the promise of eternal life. **Faith is therefore the root of the gospel of Jesus Christ.** The gospel is *"the power of God unto salvation, to everyone that **believes**",* where the *"power of God"* refers to the preaching of the cross (Romans 1:16 Emphasis added, 1 Corinthians 1:18). Therefore the root of the gospel of Jesus Christ is our *belief* that Jesus *is* the Son of God, that He died on the cross and shed His blood for the remission of our sins, and that through His sacrifice whosoever believes in Him shall have eternal life (John 3:16). Because we believe that He is who He says that He is, we will obey Him in all that He instructs us to do, for the sake of our own salvation and more importantly, out of our love for Him as our Saviour (John 14:15).

SPIRITUAL FAITH VS. CARNAL FAITH

There is such a thing as carnal faith – faith in man and in the capabilities of our own selves *without* faith in God. The Holy Spirit taught this to me:

"Faith, as you know, governs positive responses to all situations in the earthly realm. Faith in Me governs those of the spiritual. You cannot function in your anointing without faith in Me. You shall not be able to bring any action to fullness or completion if you do it doublemindedly. Whatsoever is not of faith is sin. Sin, My daughter, is rebellion against My perfect will. If you tread lightly upon a weak surface, do you make it over to the end of the room through faith alone? Or will you do so in doubt or cowardice? Neither. It is only by My Spirit, in whose power you must believe. Daughter, I teach you a new thing. For in doubt and doublemindedness, you cower and you fall through the cracks. Such is the likeness of sin: falling through the cracks, out of self-arrogance, self-faith, and self-reliance. If you rely not upon Me, then I will not carry you, for I force Myself upon no man.

Faith on its own is self-belief. Such a thing is carnal and is only of sin. Faith in Me, My daughter, is eternal. There must be a union of faith and My Holy Spirit – then comes the working of great miracles. Do not become entangled in earthly doctrines of faith in self: faith alone without faith in the Lord Most High. For what is the life of a man? Can he create himself? Can he give himself, or any other life? I am the Lord your God, and I declare that whatsoever is not of faith <u>in Me</u> is sin. No carnal faith, daughter. Faith must be of the Spirit.

Do you see now, daughter, why? If I am not in a thing, how can it last? Am I not the eternal God, your Lord Yeshua? How then can a foundation stand if it be built merely on the faith of men? For all sin shall perish. Shall not this earth pass away? What then of human faith-built structures or religions or intellectual or business-like institutions? What then of human architecture? Shall they stand? No, daughter, but whatsoever is built upon the foundation of faith in Me, the Lord Most High, it is that only which shall stand. A spiritual foundation holds and lasts forever. Whatsoever is not of faith in God is sin. In action and in transaction. In belief and in reaction. Whatsoever is not of faith in Me, shall never last, it shall never stand." (For scriptural reference, read 1 Corinthians 2:5; 3:18-21, Isaiah 65:17, Revelation 21:1).

In no way is the Lord saying that to have self-confidence is a bad thing. We must indeed be confident in our capabilities, and walk bravely and boldly in our daily lives as representatives of His Kingdom. It is when that confidence becomes arrogance, where we believe that we are self-sufficient and that we can do everything on our own, without Him - that is when we come out of His will. When we put our trust in the people around us, or in influential leaders, rather than in the All-Sufficient One - that is when our walk becomes carnal, and we are led by the flesh, and not by the Spirit of God (Romans 8:8). Such a mindset is not of God. He always draws us towards Himself, and leads us along the path of righteousness for His own name's sake (Psalm 23:3). It is a good thing to have faith, but we must ensure that our faith is in Jesus Christ.

FAITH IS A CHOICE

We must choose to believe God. As we have seen, faith is no mere word, nor is it a concept. Faith is a way of life. It determines the decisions that we make, and aligns us with our destiny. Faith causes the weak to stand strong and the deaf to hear God's voice. Faith makes the lame man walk and the dumb man speak, because he chooses to believe. Faith is a choice. Belief in who God says that He is, is not an inherent function of man. We must choose to believe that God is Almighty, all-powerful, all-sufficient, and the *only* God, and that His Word *alone* is truth, both spoken and written. Faith is no common occurrence. Who can demonstrate their belief in a person who does not exist? Don't idol worshippers – those who bow to the works of their own hands – do they not believe that their gods exist? Are not such persons still God's creation? They choose to have faith in what does not exist. Therefore, it is only by the Spirit of God that we are led to make the right choice. We henceforth choose life, because the Spirit is life (Romans 8:10, John 6:63). It is only when we choose to believe in the truth, that we shall see the evidence of the unseen realm brought to fruition before our eyes. And that is the fullness of faith.

Chapter 7

THE POWER OF LOVE

Chapter 7

THE POWER OF LOVE

And the final note that completes the song, without which the melody would be incomplete, is love. Love encapsulates the fullness of our relationship with God. It is the outer layer of the capsule that holds the medicine inside. It is the anchor to the greatest of ships on the grandest of voyages. Without love we are incomplete. Without the love of God, we are nothing. It is He who taught us how to love, because it is He who first loved us. God *is* love. And without us making a demonstration of His love, we cannot say that we also love Him.

LOVE IS

Love is patient. Love is kind. Love is not full of envy. Neither is it full of pride. Love does not behave rudely. *Love is not selfish.* It is not easily provoked. It thinks no evil of man. Love does not take pleasure in wickedness, but instead rejoices in the truth. Love does not give up. Love gives second chances. Love holds out for the good. Love endures all things. (1 Corinthians 13:4-7). I'd like to ask you to re-read the lines above, replacing the word "love" with the word "God". Isn't He beautiful? Now insert your own name and re-read it again. How did you measure up? Do you reflect God? We can see clearly that like faith, love must be demonstrated. It is not merely a word to be loosely tossed around to appeal to the emotions of the people nearest to us, when in reality, our actions speak poorly of our words. God demonstrated His love for us, by giving His only Son, Holy and sinless, as a sacrifice for us. He took all the punishment for every sin that ever was, is now and will ever be committed - punishment that we rightfully deserved (Romans 6:23) - on Himself, so that today, we may call Him Father and live with Him forever as His own (Romans 5:8). The Lord Jesus reconciled us back to the Father, so that we would not have to die, but that God would receive us once more as His children. What greater demonstration of love could there be? Love alone spoken is but an empty word. True love is not merely spoken, it is shown.

But what is love actually made of? We know what the final product should look like, but do we know its ingredients? The apostle Peter did, and he shared the recipe in 2 Peter 1: 5-7. To operate out of love takes the diligent pursuit and the disciplined practice of ***faith***. When we are able to demonstrate our belief in the King of kings by the things that we do and say in obedience to His Word, we develop the capacity to become more virtuous. ***Virtue*** is excellence of character and the demonstration of high moral standards. We learn to do what we say we are going to do, keep our promises and stand by our word. We learn the importance of speaking the truth and standing up for what is right. We learn to be impartial and non-judgmental towards others who make mistakes, or who may be of varying socio-economic and cultural backgrounds, ethnicities and educational levels. We learn to shun wickedness and to embrace righteousness. As we grow in our virtuousness, we expand in our capacity to gain ***knowledge***. This speaks not merely of the gathering of information, but of increased wisdom and understanding in the things of God, revealed to us by the Holy Spirit (See Chapter 3). As we grow in the spirit, we gain an increase of **self-control** as we submit our flesh to the will of the Spirit, and are better able to control our own carnal desires and inclinations. With more self-control comes more **patience**, not only with others, but with our own selves. We realise our own imperfections and learn to be gentle on ourselves as children of God, striving to walk the path that Jesus Christ made out for us. We will slip and fall, but He will support us and help us up. We do not have to try to please Him with rituals or rules, because He sees our hearts. Knowing that God sees our hearts, grants us the peace to become more like Him in character, that is, we have the expanded capacity for **godliness**. Faithful commitment, honour and obedience to God causes us to expand in our capacity to show and to receive **brotherly kindness**. There is a beauty of the spirit in the man who is able to be kind to a stranger, his mother, his father, an elder, his wife, his children and his leaders. To all of these things, add **the love of God** - the eternal sustenance of our being. Now, show it to others. That is the fullness of the demonstration of love.

HOW HE LOVES US

I believe that many of us know that God loves us, but we do not quite understand how much. We often question His love, and wonder if we even deserve it. Some even believe that they are not even worth being loved at all. We could not be more wrong. His love is one of great depth of the spirit. It stretches from the great expanse of eternity into our inner human core. It is so infinite and boundless that we can never truly comprehend it within our finite human form. God loves you. Let me tell you how much:

God says this –

"I the Lord your God, love you more than the human mind can comprehend. I love you by My great loving Spirit, with a love that can only be faintly understood between your spirit and My own Spirit. I the Lord your God, love you so much that I created an entire planet for you to enjoy. I build a new city of royal jewels for you to inhabit. I clothe you with robes and garments of righteousness, glory and truth. I the Lord your God, gave Myself to be sacrificed before the earth was made. I became like unto fleshly man and dwelt among you, so that you may come to know Me. I the Lord, suffered the worst persecution on the

face of the earth, in the history of man, I the Lord your God did it all for you, My little one.

I saw your little face. I saw your heart towards Me and its innocence. I the Lord your God saw your smile. Long before your parents were even conceived, did I know your name, for you are My own little one, who loves Me in return. I gave My life for you, that you may love Me and be saved. That you would come to know Me, and give Me your heart, and that you, My own, would serve Me willingly.

I love you so much that I made the universe to sustain you. The sun for energy, and the moon for the beauty of the night, to enlighten the dark, and so that you may count the seasons of time. I made every planet so that the earth would remain balanced within your solar system. I made you, My precious one, and I love you more than you will ever know. You may spend forever with Me, so that you may learn the vastness of My love for you.

I love you more than all of the books ever written. I love you more than every word ever spoken. How can you quantify the love of God towards His creation? It is like trying to number every grain of sand in every ocean of the planet, and much like quantifying the volume of air that has ever been breathed by every man who has ever lived. It is simply impossible. So great is

My love for you. Rejoice in your Father, who loves His little one. I love you, My child, and behold, I am with you always, even until the end of the earth." (For scriptural reference, read 1 John 4:9-11, Revelation 3:4; 13:8; 21:10-27, John 1:1-10, Galatians 2:20, Ephesians 1:4,5, Matthew 28:20).

No greater love exists. When we obey God, and remain under the shadow of His wings, absolutely nothing can separate us from His unending love (Romans 8:35-39). Even the angels asked Him, *"What is man, that You are mindful of him? And the son of man, that you take care of him?"* (Hebrews 2:6). They just could not figure it out. What makes us so special? *Why does God love us so much?*

"It is because no other creature has been made in My image or in My likeness. It is because you have the free will to choose to love Me. It is because I choose to dwell within your body as My temple. It is because I created you to dwell in a realm outside of the glory of heaven. A realm that is corruptible and unstable. You live on a planet, I dwell in heaven. Eternity is your destiny, should only you love Me in return. I count you as unique amongst all of My creation, there is no other creature like mankind. There is no other creature that is tripartite like I am. You are the only creature that reflects My image. How can I not love you? I indeed love all of My creation, but there is only one

THE POWER OF LOVE

mankind, to whom I have given My heart." (For scriptural reference, read Genesis 1:26-28, 1 John 5:7).

Do you see why we are so important to God? We are special amongst all of creation. No other being carries His breath and His light. God Himself placed His infinite being into a finite mortal body and walked the earth as a man, just so that we can have a relationship with Him, and not only that, but He suffered tremendous rejection and scorn, and was killed by the same men that He demonstrated His love to. He rose from the grave, nullified the power of death and obliterated all of the power of hell, just so that death would not be *our* final destination. Because He arose into glory and eternal life, so will we (2 Timothy 2:11). What great mercy. He was the first to be risen from the dead (Colossians 1:18) and so He paved the way for us, so that if we follow Him, we too shall meet Him in eternity.

Nothing was too great for our Father to do for us. He loves us so much that He wants the best for us. He will never leave us in a state of sickness of the mind or heart, spirit or body when we cry out to Him in faith. He will never abandon us when we are afraid (Deuteronomy 31:6). When we call His name, He is there. When we are lost and in trouble,

He leads us to safety (Psalm 23). He shields us from the wickedness of the world and is near to our hearts when they are heavy or broken (Psalm 34:14-18). He cries when we cry (John 11:33, 35) and rejoices when we are glad. He is pained when we turn away from Him, and is always ready to take us back, **no matter what we have ever done** (Jeremiah 4:19; Luke 15:11-32; 1 John 1:9, Psalm 103:12). No parent on earth knows the depth of love that God feels for us, but they can only imagine it. As heaven is high above the earth, that is how great His lovingkindness is to His children (Psalm 103:11). He chastens us when we go astray, but He never stays mad at us (Proverbs 3:12; Psalm 30:5). He never gives up on us, never turns away from us and never withholds His love from us (Psalm 84:11). How can we not love a God such as this?

DO YOU LOVE HIM?

If you say that you love God, do you do as He says? Our Lord Jesus said, *"He who has My commandments and keeps them, it is he who loves Me. And he who loves Me will be loved by My Father, and I will love him and manifest Myself to him"* (John 14:21). What was His commandment? *"This is My commandment, that you love one another as I have loved you"*

(John 15:12). How exactly do we do that? We have seen the components of love, and its traits that are visibly recognised, but how do we put this into practice? Jesus gave us the answer to that as well: *"And just as you want men to do to you, you also do to them likewise"* (Luke 6:31). Not only is the love that we have received from the Lord God vertical in its transmission, it is also radial in its emission. It is radial by the working of the Holy Spirit in us, being outwardly seen by those within our individual spheres of influence. This comes only through faith and obedience to His will.

> *"For this is the love of God, that we keep His commandments. And His commandments are not burdensome. For whatever is born of God overcomes the world. And this is the victory that has overcome the world—our faith"* (1 John 5:3,4).

There is a strong interconnectedness between love and faith – love requires faith to inspire it; faith requires love to drive it. How can we love God, or our even fellowman, if we do not believe in His goodness, trust in His ways, and obey His instructions? How can we demonstrate our belief in our Lord, if we do not *want* to love Him? **The link between them both is humility and obedience,** and we demonstrate them both in all that we think, say and do.

One critical requirement of us all is that we demonstrate God's love to our fellow humankind. We cannot say that we love an invisible God, yet fail to demonstrate His love to the people who we can see (1 John 4:20). It would be good to examine your heart and know your true feelings toward the people in your life, and your behaviour towards strangers. God's Word is true: you cannot love God and hate mankind (1 John 2:9-11). If you do, you must also reconsider your faith in God.

It takes a great deal of empathy to be able to demonstrate God's love towards others, including our enemies and towards people who may seem to be hard to love. It may seem to be difficult to show love to someone who could care less to reciprocate it in your direction. Someone who continuously insults you and belittles you, shows you no appreciation or hurts you, is no doubt difficult to love. Someone who is rude, manipulative or divisive surely is not a walk in the park either. (Dare I suppose that you also do not behave in such ways). You see, it may be easy to be patient, gentle, kind, temperate, or selfless towards people who we may like, but the challenge comes when we are able to show love towards those who do not love us in return. What reward is there with God if we only show love to those who love us? (Matthew 5:44-48). That makes us no different to those who may not know Jesus Christ as their Lord and Saviour. In living the lifestyle of worship, we cannot avoid this side of the path. God makes us to know in 1 John 4:7-8, that if we do not love one another, we do not know Him, because He *is* love: *"Beloved, let us love one another, for love is from God, and whoever loves has been born of God and knows God. Anyone who does not love does not know God, because God is love".*

Even as God so loved the *whole* world, not some of it, but the whole world, that He gave His Son for us, so too must we also love all men with the love that we have received from Him (John 3:16; 1 Timothy 4:10). This includes persons from varying religions and religious denominations, colours, classes, cultures and nationalities. We are to honour all men, and pay particular attention to those within the Body of Christ (1 Peter 2:17). Your life is not worth more than anyone else's in God's eyes – He is no respecter of persons (Acts 10:34,35). Neither does He take pleasure in the death of the wicked, but in their repentance (Ezekiel 18). It is for this reason, as believers in Jesus Christ, that we must give proper respect to everyone who we come into contact with. He set the example for us. What He did, so are we to do also, that we may bring honour to His name. If

Jesus found it fit to pray for those who nailed Him to the cross, how much more so can we pray for those who offend us?

WHEN YOU LOVE, YOU FORGIVE

The key, therefore to demonstrating the love of God in us, is to mortify our own fleshly ways and to be led by His Spirit. It takes circumcision of the heart, i.e. genuine repentance and inward change, that we may forfeit our natural inclination to perhaps hold a grudge, curse at an aggressor or lash out at an offender. This by no means says that we are to be hypocrites, secretly hating others, but showing them kindness on the outside. Such a thing is carnal, and is not of God. It means that we are to have our own hearts cleaned up first, so that we may act out in love, in our speech, demeanour and in our actions. When you wrong someone, make the effort to set things right, and bring peace between you both (Matthew 5:22-26). Seek the Lord's counsel and repent of your offence, whatever it may be. Genuinely apologise for what has happened, acknowledging that what you did was wrong, because saying "I'm sorry that you feel that way" is not a real apology. Remember that when you confess your sins, God is faithful and just, to forgive you of all manner of sins and cleanse you from all unrighteousness (1 John 1:9). So be easy on yourself, and release your feelings of guilt or shame. God does not condemn you. No man can either. When you are wronged, seek the Lord's counsel in handling the matter, and above all else, *forgive the one who has offended you* (Colossians 3:12-14). If however, you are continually wronged by the offender, although you must forgive, you can also make the decision to distance yourself from unkindness, acting out of Godly wisdom and not foolish commitment.

It is absolutely necessary that we forgive one another, if we are to be forgiven by God (Matthew 6:14). Unforgiveness separates us from the love of God and keeps us bound to the one who has brought on the offence. It is a burden and a heavy yoke to carry. It stems from our own emotional bondage and can be rooted in pride. Forgiveness is not always simple or easy to do, especially when a person's actions may seem to be absolutely unforgivable. But let God repay them for what they have done, and for the sake of your own mental and emotional health, and most importantly, your salvation, you *must* forgive. No matter what, release it to God – He will repay (Romans 12:19).

Begin the process of forgiveness by praying for those who hurt you. The Lord taught me that that is the key to forgiving others who are hard to forgive. When we pray for those who have offended or hurt us, out of sincerity and surrender to God, we begin to view those individuals from a heavenly perspective. We begin to see the side of them that God sees – what He loves about them, and we then begin to see them as being separate from their actions. God will often reveal the spiritual influence behind a person's actions or behaviour and teach you how to pray about it. Remember that all human interaction, all communication, every personal experience is of spiritual influence. Open your eyes to the supernatural and begin to see the works of the enemy behind the unkind actions of men. We have God's Spirit inside of us, therefore we know that we are not warring against anything that we can see. Begin to separate persons from their actions and pray accordingly. If they remain unchanged while you yet must interact with them, maintain your distance and your dignity in Christ.

MORE THAN WORDS

When you say that you love someone, mean it by the things that you do. Too often within the Body of Christ, the word "love" is loosely spoken and hardly demonstrated. If you love your brother or sister, then visit them when they are ill, call them if they go missing, support them with their business or help them to find a job. Check in on the widows and be patient with the elderly. Don't gossip about them or tell lies about them. Don't backstab them for a title or position in the church, or seat them at the back of the room because their car is old or their offerings are not as large as yours are. If you say that you love your congregation, then get to know who they are, meet them at their point of need and apologise when you know that a member is hurting because of your actions toward them. Practise what you preach, treat everyone in your flock with equal respect, and go after a sheep when it goes missing. Keep their secrets and speak the *truth* when you minister to them. Don't use the microphone or the pulpit as a weapon to assault with words, victimize those who may disagree with you, or manipulate the Scriptures to send a personal message. This behaviour is ungodly and God takes note of all of it, to reward each of us according to the works of our hands (Ezekiel 34:2-16; Jeremiah 23:1-4; Job 34:11).

CARNAL LOVE VS. SPIRITUAL LOVE

In the previous chapter, we saw the difference between spiritual faith and carnal faith. The same applies to love. This is what the Lord taught to me:

"What is carnal love? Is it not the lust of the flesh? It is the inherent desire of a man to show kindness out of his heart toward another human being, devoid of the counsel or guide of My Spirit. It is self-motivated and selfish in nature, for it seeks to satisfy self. A feel-good sensation that man <u>feels</u> to share affection in the flesh. It feels good, in that it appeals to the flesh. When love in a man is out of the love of My Spirit, it is demonstrated out of love for Me. It connects to Me, and honours My name. All things are done unto My glory and not to the glory of self.

Can a man complete himself by his external actions toward another? There are not enough tasks on the earth that will ever be completed, if a man seeks to satisfy his own heart. This will lead him to loneliness and emptiness when he realises that such a devotion can never complete him. A vacuum exists inside of every man, that only My Spirit can fill. Only My love can make you whole. Not the demonstration of kindness from a human motive, but only out of obedience to My will, that My name be glorified. Such is the difference between the love of the flesh and the love of the Spirit. One seeks to satisfy self, the other seeks to glorify Me." (For scriptural reference, read 1 John 2:15-17, Romans 8:5-13, 1 Corinthians 10:31).

The Lord revealed this quite clearly to me. It does not matter what you do on this earth for the sake of showing love to others. If it does not bring glory to God, then your intention is a selfish one, even simply for the motive that it makes *you* feel satisfied, complete, or like a better person (whether consciously or unconsciously). In all that we do, we must do it to the glory of God. This includes showing love. So be sure to examine your motives for demonstrating love to others. Are you being led by the Holy Spirit? Are you doing it out of your love and faith in God, and in obedience to His will? Or is it something that you do because it feels good to do it? The works of the flesh can never please Him. Our love for Him always will.

Chapter 8

OBEDIENCE IS BETTER THAN SACRIFICE

Chapter 8

OBEDIENCE IS BETTER THAN SACRIFICE

The lifestyle of worship is centred on obedience to God. In the previous chapters, I have mentioned obedience a number of times, so now let us take a deeper look into its value and its importance in having a relationship with our Father.

GOD REQUIRES OUR OBEDIENCE

What is obedience? It is the ready compliance with an order or request made by someone with a measure of authority over you. It takes a great deal of humility and respect for the one making the request, and the submission of the one in compliance establishes the order of leadership. When we know that God is speaking to us, we ought to immediately obey His commands. Our delay or refusal to comply may be considered to be disobedience or insubordination, and can even border on rebellion. Many times, we do not see the value of obeying God. Neither do we see its grave importance. We assume that when He speaks, it is up to us to choose whether or not we want to obey Him, and if we do choose to obey him, we do so on our own time. And for the most part, we are surely right to think so. But it is the choice that we make to immediately comply with God's instructions through His *rhema* word, *logos* Word, a dream, vision, angelic message or a prophetic word, that causes Him to draw nearer to us, and to trust us as His children and as His friends. A good parent gives instructions to a child for the purpose of the growth and development of their character, the enhancement of their capabilities and skill and for the improvement of their understanding. A parent's instructions can be for the child's own safety and protection, and for their overall wellbeing. The submission and resulting obedience of the child demonstrates honour and love for their parent. So it is with us and the Lord. It is a basic test of readiness for servanthood in the will and the way of God, if we prove ourselves worthy through obedience.

Let us take a look at this account in the first book of Samuel, chapters 10-15. The people of Israel began to lose faith in God through their fear of neighbouring armies. They envied the governmental structures of the heathen nations surrounding them, and so they demanded that the Lord give them a king to rule over them. This displeased God, of course, because *He* was their King. Nevertheless, He decided to give them what they asked for. He sent His prophet Samuel to find this king that they so earnestly desired. Saul, son of Kish, a Benjamite, fit the mould. He was the tallest and most handsome amongst all of the people, and his heart was lowly and pure. He came from humble beginnings and sought no position of leadership at all. God chose Saul to be king over His people, and *anointed him for His service*. He transformed His heart into one that He could use and made Him into a great leader. He said these words to the people upon Saul's coronation through Prophet Samuel:

> *"If you fear the Lord and serve Him and obey His voice, and do not rebel against the commandment of the Lord, then both you and the king who reigns over you will continue following the Lord your God. However, if you do not obey the voice of the Lord, but rebel against the commandment of the Lord, then the hand of the Lord will be*

against you, as it was against your fathers" (Chapter 12:14,15).

Surely Saul would obey the words of God's prophet. And He did. Saul was more than honoured to be chosen by God for this great service. He would make history and be remembered for all time as the very first king of Israel. Whatever Prophet Samuel instructed Him to do, He did it. This was until Saul became overwhelmed with his own authority and forgot that it was God who had made him king. He decided to do his own thing, lead the army his way, and repeatedly disobeyed the instructions of Prophet Samuel. He became arrogant, self-sufficient and filled with the cement of self. Pride became his downfall. Disobedience became his detriment. In a final act of blatant disobedience to the instructions of God, Saul was cast down in the sight of the Lord and was stripped of the presence of the Spirit of God, the legacy of his rulership, and his favour in the eyes of God's prophet.

The Lord regretted that He had chosen Saul as king over His people, and so He sought after another who would seek His own heart. One who would serve Him with honour and all humility. Saul was replaced by another whom God had chosen, whom He knew would seek to obey Him. Through Saul's disobedience to God, *he was replaced* by David, a shepherd boy and musician, who later became the greatest king of Israel through His obedience to the Lord his God.

There is enough from that account to teach us all a very valuable lesson. No matter the grandeur of our accomplishments or how fantastic we perceive our own selves to be, God values our humble obedience more than anything else. His ways are not our own, neither are His thoughts similar to ours (Isaiah 55:8,9). Who can imagine the mind of God? When He instructs us to do something, it is because He has a purpose for doing so, and it always turns out to be for our own good. He will never lead us astray. We may not always understand why He instructs us to do something, or why He allows certain things to happen, but we must trust that because He is God, He sees the bigger picture, and He already knows the outcome. We must do our part to obey His Word.

The difference between King Saul and King David was their heart condition. Saul lost sight of the Lord and became like a god in his own eyes. He justified his actions through his own reasoning and acted out of pride. David saw himself as a man in need of divine counsel, assistance and protection. He loved the God of Israel, and feared Him tremendously. He never forgot who He was, and the Lord never forgot who he was. This is not to say that David never disobeyed God. Many times he erred. But his heart was ever repentant towards the Lord, and God in His mercy never forsook Him. He knew that David's heart was sincere. The Lord humbled him, and made him a shepherd of sheep, so that he would know how to lead a nation of people. Can we not also learn a lesson from Kings David and Saul?

OBEDIENCE BRINGS REWARD

"Blessed are those who hear the word of God and keep it!" (Luke 11:28). To keep God's Word means to honour and obey it. There is great reward in keeping God's Word. Who can say that they are a child of God, if they do not follow their Parent's instructions? Too often as believers in Jesus Christ, we claim that we know Him, yet besides not spending sufficient time in His presence, we do not do what He says to do. We live lives of dishonour before the Lord, morphing His incorruptible nature into a God who is okay with our sin (Romans 1:21-32). We falsify His holiness by creating a god to suit ourselves, calling him by the name of

"Jesus", when in reality we are only bringing reproach to His name and disobeying His unchanging Word. To know the real Jesus Christ is to love Him, and to love Him is to obey His instructions. He is not a God who compromises to suit our comfortable unrighteousness. It is we who are transformed to suit His holiness. The Bible says that the only way that we will know that we are in Christ and that our salvation is secure is if we keep God's commandments (1 John 2:3-5). **It also says that not everyone who names Jesus Christ as their Lord will enter into heaven, *unless* they have obeyed the Father, by doing His will (Matthew 7: 21-13).** We know that the ultimate reward for keeping God's commands is eternal life – living forever with Him in His Kingdom. But there is also much reward while we are yet on the earth.

OBEDIENCE BRINGS PROMOTION

For everything there is a time and a season. Throughout our lives we will pass through various seasons of giving and receiving, sowing and reaping (Ecclesiastes 3:1-8). And every season is the predecessor for the next one on its way. In each season, God gives us instructions on how we should invest the resources that He has divinely blessed us with, such as our *time*, gifts, talents, abilities and our finances, in preparation for the next stage of our lives. When we sow these things in obedience, we sow in perfect synchronisation with heaven's timing. And so, when the time for harvest comes, we will reap the reward of what we have sown (Galatians 6:7). God has plans to increase us, expand our territories and prosper us. When we do as He says, when He says to do it, we will surely receive the blessing that is released from heaven in response to our action of faith. If we hesitate in doubt, or fail to act because of defiance, then we would miss our harvest, and reap nothing good when the time for receiving comes.

BLESSING OR CURSE?

Remember the link between the spiritual and the physical: as it is in the spirit, so it is manifested in the natural. When God releases a word in the spirit realm, whether over our own personal lives, or even over a nation of people, our response in the physical determines the manner of the manifestation of that word. Let me explain. If we choose to respond with immediate compliance through faith, we will receive what God has intended to be a blessing upon our lives. If we respond with unbelief or defiance, then that is when the enemy gains legal ground to intervene in our lives. He gains a legal foothold to oppose God's word, possibly bringing on delay, oppression, frustration, physical harm or injury, and even loss of possessions, status or inheritance. This is laid out clearly in Deuteronomy chapter 28. Moses tells the children of Israel:

> *"Now it shall come to pass, if you diligently obey the voice of the Lord your God, to observe carefully all His commandments which I command you today, that the Lord your God will set you high above all nations of the earth. And all these blessings shall come upon you and overtake you, because you obey the voice of the Lord your God"* (verses 1 and 2).

He then outlines a number of beautiful promises of blessings that God intends to bestow upon them. However, he also outlines the consequences of disobedience followed by a detailed description of such penalties:

> *"But it shall come to pass, if you do not obey the voice of the Lord your God, to observe carefully all His commandments and His statutes which I command you today, that all these curses will come upon you and overtake you"* (verse 15).

These Scriptures surely were demonstrated throughout history. When the children of Israel chose to live in humble obedience unto the Lord (for example, Joshua, 1 Kings 1-10), they were beautifully blessed. When they chose to live in purposeful disobedience to Him, they were gravely cursed (for instance, Judges, Jeremiah). Surely we are now under the new covenant of Jesus Christ, but the Kingdom policy regarding obedience and disobedience still stands: *"the wages of sin is death,* (the ultimate curse for living in disobedience), *but the gift of God is eternal life in Christ Jesus our Lord"* (Romans 6:23). If we are citizens of His Kingdom, then these rules apply to us.

Thankfully, God is so merciful and gracious, that even when we do disobey Him, which we all do at some point, He does not hesitate to give us the opportunity to repent and to make right with Him. He is not a harsh task master or an unfeeling, iron-faced ruler who is impossible to please. He does not threaten us or seek to instill fear into our hearts, should we ever make a mistake. Neither does He require us to carry out empty acts of penitence which have no eternal value. He only requires that we acknowledge when we have done wrong, repent of it, and in learning our lesson, do what is right in His sight (1 John 1:9). Just as a remorseful child would do. It is therefore up to us to do what we know would be pleasing to our Father.

DISOBEDIENCE LEADS OTHERS TO DEATH; OBEDIENCE, TO LIFE

When you represent Jesus Christ, other persons, particularly unbelievers within your sphere of influence, hold you to a particular standard of righteousness. When you walk in disobedience, it shows them (who do not know better), that it is okay to live in sin. In their eyes if you who are "righteous" walk in sin, then so can they. If you who are a Christian live in a similar manner to they who are in the world, then what difference would it make whether or not they followed after Jesus Christ? A deceptively blurred line is formed, distorting their perception of darkness and light. In their eyes, both light and dark merge into shades of grey, and there forms no clear distinction between either realm. Disobedience is like a poison to their own hearts and minds, and leads them not unto repentance, but unto death. Would you then be responsible for leading others into sin? (Romans 14:21).

Obedience leads others to life. For when you walk in obedience, your lifestyle is like unto a beacon that shines the light along the path for others to follow. By the example that you have set, the unbeliever can be led to choose the path of righteousness, repentance and eternal life. The distinction between darkness and light becomes clearer, and the choice of lifestyle becomes more easily defined. Therefore whether you walk in obedience or disobedience as a representative of Christ Jesus, you affect your sphere of influence. Be conscious of how your lifestyle influences the people around you, that you do not lead them away from God, and into sin.

ON EARTH AS IT IS IN HEAVEN

Just as the Kingdom of God has a structure of government and authority that we must submit to, so the Lord has allowed on the earth. As we obey Him and submit to His Lordship, so has He instructed that we also obey those in authority over us on the earth. This applies to government authority and organizational leadership, including the church. The book of Romans chapter 13 says:

> *"Let every soul be subject to the governing authorities. For there is no authority except from God, and the authorities that exist are appointed by God"* (Verse 1).

> *"Therefore whoever resists the authority resists the ordinance of God, and those who resist will bring judgment on themselves"* (Verse 2).

> *"Render therefore to all their due: taxes to whom taxes are due, customs to whom customs, fear to whom fear, honour to whom honour"* (Verse 7). Similarly, you may also read 1 Peter 2:13-17.

God desires that we always submit to all manner of authority. It is He who lifts up leaders, and He who casts them down (Psalm 75:7; Daniel 2:21). The heart of the king is always in His hand, to do or to allow whatever He wishes, whether the king be saved or not (Proverbs 21:1). We do not always understand His ways, but we must always trust that there is a purpose behind His works. It is our job, as humble servants, to do as He says. Whether authority is good or evil, as citizens of the Kingdom of God, we *must* submit and obey. We ought to remember that although we are not *of* this world, we do live *in* it. There is no rebellion against authority in God's Kingdom (not anymore, since the enemy was cast out). We therefore must not rebel against authority on the earth.

Even if you belong to an organisation that has cruel or unkind leadership, in obedience to our Lord Jesus Christ, we then must submit and obey the leaders in charge. This is certainly not easy to do, particularly when your leader is incorrect about a matter, unjust, uncouth, or unfair in their behaviour and handling of it. Still, submit and obey. God sees all things, and as He is a God of justice and righteousness, He will reward all men according to their works (Psalm 9:8). When we submit to morally unjust or cruel leadership, there is great reward with God, for He sees that our hearts are fixed on honouring *Him*. Apostle Peter taught us this as well:

> *"Servants, be submissive to your masters with all fear, not only to the good and gentle, but also to the harsh. For this is com-mendable, if because of conscience toward God one endures grief, suffering wrongfully.*
>
> *For what credit is it if, when you are beaten for your* ***faults****, you take it patiently?* ***But when you do good and suffer, if you take it patiently, this is commendable before God****. For to this you were called, because Christ also suffered for us, leaving us an example, that you should follow His steps:*

> '*Who committed no sin, nor was deceit found in His mouth'; Who, when He was reviled, did not revile in return; when He suffered, He did not threaten, but committed Himself to Him who judges righteously*" (1 Peter 2:18-23 Emphasis added).

Our Lord Jesus Christ set the perfect example for us to follow in every way, including submission to earthly authority. If He, who was very much God and very much man, who had the power to obliterate the political structure of the day, submitted to man-made earthly authority, even unto death, then so can we. The student is not above his teacher (Matthew 10:24). As He obeyed, so must we obey also.

This is not to say that you should allow yourself to be abused either. Whether emotionally, physically or otherwise, you do have the right to be treated respectfully as a human being. Additionally, if the one under whose authority you are, is leading you to sin against God, then you must stand for what is right, and/or remove yourself from under such authority (Daniel 3). Do this not by rebellion, but by making the decision to honour God more than man (Acts 4:18; 5:29). God's will is not that we disobey Him so that we may please mankind. It is therefore important to seek the Lord's counsel in knowing how to proceed under such circumstances. Allow the Lord to search your own heart as well, and see whether there is any fault in your own character that you may need to repent of. In all things use the wisdom that He so freely gives to us all.

Chapter 9

THE SECRET TO VICTORIOUS LIVING

Chapter 9

THE SECRET TO VICTORIOUS LIVING

"Righteousness exalts a nation, but sin is as a reproach unto any people" (Proverbs 14:34).

Why is sin like a reproach to the ones covered in it? Why would sin bring on rebuke, scorn, disapproval or reprimand? Whose reprimand? The Lord's. The Lord hates the very appearance of sin. It is likened unto a putrid, deathly odour to His nostrils. An offence that *must* be removed. Surely sin cannot abide in His presence. But the righteousness of the righteous, is likened unto a sweet-smelling savour. It is a sacrifice that we make which pleases Him greatly (Psalm 4:5).

As believers in Jesus Christ, our lives must be covered in His blood, and free from sin. Though temptations will continually come, because we are all sinners, we must therefore persistently be made clean by His blood. What am I saying? It takes continuous spiritual effort to overcome the offences of this life, so that our lives may be pleasing to the One who saved us from sin. Offences will come in a myriad of temptations, unforeseeable situations, diseases and ill health. There may be some family members who become helplessly lost and other loved ones who attack your faith. There may be challenges in the home and in the workplace; there may be financial loss and debt. There may be opposition from unbelievers whose intentions are to belittle your God, turn others against you, or to convert you to their own faith. You may be segregated against, gossiped about or betrayed by the ones you trust. Assassination attempts may be made on your character and your reputation, attempts to ruin your name. There may be challenges in your marriage, your friendships and your ministry. Battles to be fought daily. They seem to never end. How can we possibly overcome these daily roughages, without falling into sin? How can we possibly be victorious in this life that we live on the earth, as sojourners through a dark world filled with the blinding lights of falsehoods?

THE SECRET REVEALED

God taught me that it *is* possible for us to be victorious, and it begins and ends with His presence. Victorious living is not the pursuit and attainment of nice things, or the ability to maintain a positive outlook when you go through trials. Neither is it merely the proper application of personal development and empowerment skills – though these do have their place. **Victorious living is the carrying forth of the presence and the glory of God from the spirit to the natural, which transcends into every area of our lives.** It is manifested in the supernatural ability to overcome every possible stone that the enemy casts at us, by the divine intervention of God, because of the manifest presence of His Holy Spirit.

The Lord Jesus taught me the secret to victorious living:

"Readiness for battle is merely the ascension into My glory, for it is My glory that equips you to combat the enemy, and it is My presence that grants My servants the victory. How do you ascend, My daughter? With worship! The lifestyle that leads to the <u>act</u> of worship in <u>spirit</u> and in truth; My truth, which is the Word of God that is pure. There are many elements of worship, My dear daughter, and worship often precedes warfare.

You cannot worship in the flesh. The flesh cannot please Me, for the flesh signifies death and carnality. The Spirit is life. I am life. Therefore, when you live by the Spirit, it is then where you live a life of worship. That then brings you to the <u>act</u> of worship.

Only then, in clean garments will you ascend into My divine presence, and there is where I shall equip you to fight. For from there, I send you forth, and go with you to battle, and only then can you defeat your enemies. Remember when My people in times past, went to war with the Ark of My covenant. When My presence was with them, they gained the victory. When they were in unrighteousness, though the Ark be present, I was not, and so they lost and were defeated by their enemies. Therefore My daughter, **it is righteous living that allows you to ascend in worship, then go forth in My presence, and then you shall always be victorious.**

Listen not to lies and false teachings about victorious living. What is victory without My presence? It cannot exist. For it is I who grant the victory unto my faithful servants. It is I who fight your battles, and it is I who gain ground on your behalf. On your own, you fight but the flesh. Remember My Word: It is not by might, nor by power, but by My Spirit, says the Lord." (For scriptural reference, read Romans 8:8, 1 Samuel 4-7, Exodus 14:14, Zechariah 4:6).

SHOW ME YOUR GLORY

We have just learned that it is the glory of God which equips us to fight, and it is His presence that enables us to be victorious over our enemies. But before we move forward, what exactly is the glory of God? And why do we need His presence? Let us firstly understand the greatness of God's glory.

The glory of the Lord is the evidence of the presence of His Spirit. It can be both visible and invisible. God's glory is not independent of His being — wherever He is, there is His glory also. It is much like what is understood as the human aura. There are scientists and various religions which teach that living creatures carry an invisible field of energy that radiates off of them. It is an air or quality which surrounds a person or thing that is distinctly recognizable, yet is intangible. Some may say that a certain individual gives off a particular vibe. Here we focus not on the teachings of such theories or religions. But for the sake of comparison of this concept, we certainly can liken the glory of God to being a resonating field of energy that comes off of the presence of His Person.

There are two dimensions of God's glory: His externally radiating glory and His glory that moves and is transformed. The glory that radiates from His being is His light, His brilliance, His magnificent splendour. This manner of His glory is seen. It is what Ezekiel saw (Ezekiel 1:26,27). The prophets Daniel and Isaiah saw His glory (Daniel 7:9,10; Isaiah 6:1). Even the disciples Peter, James and John saw His glory that shone as a light on the mount of transfiguration (Matthew 17:1,2; Luke 9:28-31). That is His *Shekinah*. It falls not. It moves not. It simply is.

The glory that moves, that falls and is transformed is His *kavod*. That is the smoke and the fire that the children of Israel saw in the wilderness (Exodus 13:21). That is what moves through His temple (Ezekiel 43:5, Revelation 15:8). It is like thick smoke that engulfs us, or a heavy force that is laid gently upon us. It is His *kavod* that the saints carry forth upon the earth. God's glory is both where He is, and it goes wherever He sends it. When we ascend into His holy place through worship, we come directly into contact with His glory. In His Holy temple, where He dwells, His *kavod* fills the rooms. It is usually His *kavod* that we experience in worship.

God is like a powerful magnet and His glory is much like a strong magnetic field that draws the righteous nearer to Him, and repels all manner of wickedness. The beings in this magnetic field all gain a magnetic charge. And so the closer that we move toward Him when we worship Him, adore Him and actively seek His face, the more magnetically charged we become. His energy rubs off onto us, and when we come out from His Holy presence, we remain with the charge of His magnet. Descending into the earthly realm, all things that belong to Him are drawn toward us, and those that are not His are forcefully repelled. This is what it means to be walking in the glory of God. Through our repentance of sin and sacrifice of righteousness, we are able to spiritually ascend using the vehicle of worship, into God's Holy place and come into His glorious presence. The more frequently that we do this, the more constant, and ever increasing is His glory upon our lives. The further we move away from God, through unrighteousness, or by failing to make the effort to worship Him in the spirit, the weaker His glory upon us becomes. It then becomes easier for us to live by the flesh and hence fall into sin. We walk around as dull magnets, with little to no charge. It is therefore imperative that we spend time worshipping the Lord in spirit and in truth, so that His glory may be upon us. Moses did this, as he beheld God's glory face to face (Exodus 33:11). When we come into the presence of the Lord, we carry forth His glory wherever we go. That is how we become carriers of His glory.

For the saints of God, His glory is much like our personal armour (Isaiah 4:5). We know that there is the basic spiritual armour of salvation, righteousness, truth, peace, faith and the Word of God (Ephesians 6:11-17). But there is also the heavenly armour of the glory of God that equips us for battle against an unseen enemy. This is a spiritual occurrence. God gives us His glory so that we may carry it forth as a personal force field. The enemy sees it. He knows it all too well. When clothed with the glory of God, and we speak forth with authority in the name of Jesus, we can command a demon to flee, and behold miracles of healing and deliverance before our eyes. They flee not because they fear us, but because they fear Jesus, and when we are clothed in His glory, when they see us, it is as if they see Him, for they know that He is with us. When they hear us speak, it is as if they hear Him, because they know that His Spirit is inside of us. Apostle Peter walked in the glory of the Lord, and demons fled if only by the casting of his shadow (Acts 5:12-15). His shadow itself bore no power, but the glory of the

Lord was so great upon him, through spending time in His presence, that as far as Peter's shadow could reach, that is how far the glory of the Lord emanated from Him.

To be clear, *the glory of God is different to what we may know as the anointing*. And the difference is this: the glory of God is the evidence of His presence (as we have just seen), whereas the anointing is the demonstration of what His glory can do, i.e., what can happen when He is present. It is the demonstration of God's power in His presence. Think of it this way: you are baking a cake, and you pre-heat the oven before you place your batter inside to bake. God is like the pre-heated oven. The heat that you feel when you open the oven door is His glory. The transforming agent that changes the raw batter into a cooked cake is His anointing. His presence is His Person – the manifestation of His Spirit. The radiating energy that comes off of Him is His glory, and the demonstration of His power to transform, heal, deliver and strengthen is His anointing.

IN HIS PRESENCE THERE IS VICTORY

When we ascend into God's holy presence in worship, He speaks. There is a time to open our mouths in worship, and there is a time to be silent. The Holy Spirit will prompt us to be quiet when we enter into the holy place, because it is there where we gain revelation, strategy, guidance, direction and correction from the Lord. He speaks to us in the inner man by His Spirit and equips us for success in our daily lives. It is in the holy place where we gain the blueprint of God's plans for us, and instructions for successfully carrying out our assignments on the earth. It is in the holy place where we gain spiritual tenacity, strength and boldness. We become refreshed and spiritually renewed, and we become ready to face the challenges of the world.

So we see that in His presence, God clothes us with the armour of His glory, and imparts to us divine insight and strategy. That is not all. He also comes with us as we leave His heavenly realm and return into the earthly plane, to grant us the victory. You see, His Spirit goes before us, stands with us and is within us. And only He has the power to defeat spiritual opposition. You have read in Chapter 4 how God fights our battles in the spirit realm, and how we experience the resulting victory in the natural. His presence is indomitable, and when we go forth with His presence, no weapon formed against us can ever succeed. Not against our relationships, self-esteem, identity, health, careers, finances, households, ministry – nothing. When God's presence goes with us, our victory is secured. I'd like to encourage you to read 1 Samuel 4-7, which gives an amazing demonstration of the power of the presence of the Lord, and our helplessness without it.

Our Lord Jesus Christ is the perfect example of living victoriously. He went forth in the glory *and* the presence of God. Jesus spent an essential amount of time in the presence of God. He sought the Father always in His moments of solitude, and through prayer, praise and worship. It is therefore safe to infer that He too ascended spiritually into the presence of God the Father, and received strength and counsel for the road ahead. He came out from the secret place to face the world every day clothed in the glory of the Lord. The Spirit of God abided with Him, and wherever He went, there too was the presence of God. Jesus was always ready to face His enemies, and He did so victoriously. For in all things, He gave honour unto the Father.

The key to living in the glory and the presence of God therefore, is righteousness; living a life of holiness unto the Lord. If we choose to worship the Lord with sullied souls or dirty hands, clouded minds or unrepentant hearts, then we would not spiritually ascend anywhere, and our worship would be carnal. We can jump and dance and sing all we want to – it would only be in the flesh. Righteousness is the only means whereby we can come into the presence of a holy God, become covered with His glory, receive His word of instruction, and go forth into the earth with His presence unto victory.

If, like David, we ask our Lord Jesus:

"Lord, who may abide in Your tabernacle?
Who may dwell in Your holy hill?"

Then He will say:

"He who walks uprightly,
And works righteousness,
And speaks the truth in his heart;
He who does not backbite with his tongue,
Nor does evil to his neighbour,
Nor does he take up a reproach against his friend;

In whose eyes a vile person is despised,
But he honours those who fear the Lord;
He who swears to his own hurt and does not change;
He who does not put out his money at usury,
Nor does he take a bribe against the innocent.
He who does these things shall never be moved"
(Psalm 15).

Chapter 10

DO NOT FORGET YOUR GOD

Chapter 10

DO NOT FORGET YOUR GOD

"Oh, how great is Your goodness,
Which You have laid up for those who fear You,
Which You have prepared for those who trust in You
In the presence of the sons of men!"
(Psalm 31:19).

Declare the faithfulness of our God, for He has surely bestowed His goodness upon His chosen, and has laid up eternal blessings for the saints who call Him Father. Do not be ashamed to testify of His merciful grace upon your life; the grace that you have witnessed with your own eyes; the grace that you are even yet to behold. Never forget the things that He has done and the miracles that He has promised to do. Never forget His goodness. Never forget your God.

A SURE REWARD

The lifestyle of worship is one of reward, for the Lord is a rewarder of them who diligently seek Him (Hebrews 11:6). When we live a life of worship unto the Lord, that is exactly what we do. We seek Him daily, that we may know Him and obey His Word when we find Him (Jeremiah 29:13). God feels for us, and His heart is moved by our efforts to follow after Him, no matter what. Through the trials and the tests, the hardships and the pain, the joy and the laughter and the celebration again, take comfort that your efforts have not been in vain. We are sure to receive our reward.

Deuteronomy chapter 8 is one of my favorite chapters in the Bible. It has been a life lesson for me, and forms a great part of who I am today. This is what Moses said to the children of Israel as they were about to come out of the wilderness and cross over into the Promised Land:

> *"All the commandments which I command thee this day shall ye observe to do, that ye may live, and multiply, and go in and possess the land which the Lord sware unto your fathers. And **thou shalt remember all the way which the Lord thy God led thee these forty years in the wilderness, to***

humble thee, and to prove thee, to know what was in thine heart, whether thou wouldest keep his commandments, or no. And he humbled thee, and suffered thee to hunger, and fed thee with manna, which thou knewest not, neither did thy fathers know; that he might make thee know that **man doth not live by bread only, but by every word that proceedeth out of the mouth of the Lord doth man live.** *Thy raiment waxed not old upon thee, neither did thy foot swell, these forty years. Thou shalt also consider in thine heart, that,* **as a man chasteneth his son, so the Lord thy God chasteneth thee.**

"Therefore thou shalt keep the commandments of the Lord thy God, to walk in his ways, and to fear him. For the Lord thy God bringeth thee into a good land, a land of brooks of water, of fountains and depths that spring out of valleys and hills; a land of wheat, and barley, and vines, and fig trees, and pomegranates; a land of oil olive, and honey; a land wherein thou shalt eat bread without scarceness, thou shalt not lack any thing in it; a land whose stones are iron, and out of whose hills thou mayest dig brass. **When thou hast eaten and art full, then thou shalt bless the Lord thy God for the good land which he hath given thee.**

"Beware that thou forget not the Lord thy God, in not keeping his commandments, and his judgments, and his

***statutes**, which I command thee this day: lest when thou hast eaten and art full, and hast built goodly houses, and dwelt therein; and when thy herds and thy flocks multiply, and thy silver and thy gold is multiplied, and all that thou hast is multiplied; then thine heart be lifted up, and thou forget the Lord thy God, which brought thee forth out of the land of Egypt, from the house of bondage; who led thee through that great and terrible wilderness, where-in were fiery serpents, and scorpions, and drought, where there was no water; who brought thee forth water out of the rock of flint; who fed thee in the wilderness with manna, which thy fathers knew not, **that he might humble thee, and that he might prove thee, to do thee good at thy latter end; and thou say in thine heart, My power and the might of mine hand hath gotten me this wealth**.*

*"But thou shalt **remember the Lord thy God: for it is he that giveth thee power to get wealth**, that he may establish his covenant which he sware unto thy fathers, as it is this day. And it shall be, **if thou do at all forget the Lord thy God, and walk after other gods, and serve them, and worship them, I testify against you this day that ye shall surely perish**. As the nations which the Lord destroyeth before your face, so shall ye perish; **because ye would not be obedient unto the voice of the Lord your God**."* (KJV. Emphasis added).

As children of Spiritual Israel, this indeed applies to all of us. Many times in our quest to serve the Lord, He does in fact allow us to go through hardships, so that He may bring out the best in us. He puts us through the fire to melt off the dross, so that what remains *in us* is as pure gold. He allows us to be shaken so that whatsoever can be shaken will be, and what remains afterward is that which cannot be removed (Hebrews 12:26, 27). He tests us to see whether we would remain faithful to Him. He tries us to see whether He could trust us to steward the small things, and whether we would turn away from Him the moment things change for the better, or on the contrary, lose faith in Him if things get worse. These tests are meant to shape us into the sons and daughters that we were created to be, and to bring us to a place where we absolutely must rely on our God. They are meant to shape us into worthy vessels that God can use for His purpose on the earth. They are not meant for our demise. When we see our hardships as burdens rather than as learning experiences, we begin to complain – *and that is when we fail.* The lesson must then begin all over again. We pass these tests by faithful obedience to God, by humbly trusting in Him and by standing aside to allow Him to demonstrate that He is God. When we pass these tests the result is always the great reward of spiritual growth and maturation, and we also receive the blessings of His fulfilled promises.

It is always easy for us to make promises to God when things are challenging. "Lord, if you heal me, I'll never smoke another cigarette again". "Lord please increase me. I promise to pay my tithes when I get a bigger salary". "Lord, I need You, my marriage is falling apart! I promise to be faithful to my spouse from now on". And the Lord is faithful to attend unto our cries, sometimes testing us to see whether we would remember Him when our situation improves (Psalm 66:12-20). When He has healed your body, do you give Him the credit, or do you praise your doctor and the treatment that he/she prescribed? Do you keep your promise of repentance from using harmful substances, or do you forget about God and return to it? When He has increased your finances, do you glorify Him by putting it to good use, or do your priorities shift to suddenly finding more things to spend on? Do you keep your promise of paying your tithes that are rightfully His, and do you honour Him with your increase? (Proverbs 3:9). When He has softened the heart of your spouse and brought reconciliation between you both, do you acknowledge His work, or do you thank your marriage counsellor, and pat yourself on the back for being so good at making up? Do you keep your promise of repentance from adultery, or do your eyes begin to wander, and your heart become filled with lust for another? Here we see a connection between forgetting the goodness of our God and falling back into sin. When we acknowledge His works, glorify Him and direct all praises toward Him, we are indeed kept from returning to do the things we once did, which we so earnestly repented from. The Bible says that God will keep us in perfect peace if we keep Him in all of our thoughts (Isaiah 26:3).

When our lives improve, and we become comfortable in our state of prosperity, it is easy to forget the miracles that our Lord Jesus Christ has done in our lives, and where He has taken us from. It becomes easy to forget that it is He who gave us the idea for our business, it is He who sent the clients our way, and it is He who helped us to get the job done. You may say that this can never happen to you, but if it could happen to the children of Israel who frequently forgot the goodness of the Lord just as quickly as He would demonstrate it, then it can certainly happen to us. We in many ways are not much different to them. The cause of this forgetfulness is pride (see Chapter 3). When we become so haughtily self-sufficient that we desire to exclaim before strangers and friends "Look what I've done!" we forget that we are not our own, and that we can do nothing eternally significant by our own strength. It is not by *your* own strength that your baby is born healthy. It is not by *your* own gifts that people encounter the Lord when *you* lead worship. Neither is it by *your* laying on of hands or the prayers that *you* pray that your brother/sister receives his/her healing. It is only by the Spirit of our Lord Jesus Christ that we can do all things (Philippians 4:13).

Let us therefore avoid the tragedy of forgetting the goodness of our God, by having an attitude of gratefulness. Giving thanks to God in all things, brings His goodness to our remembrance, keeps us from being prideful and from returning to past sins. It also keeps us from complaining and from being discontented. When we are sincerely grateful to the Lord for what He has done, is doing, and will do, we place Him first. He is held above all things and our hearts are set on Him, because we love Him. The lifestyle of worship is therefore one of humility and gratitude.

I will share this with you:

"Write the words of prosperity along the corridors of your mind. Write the blessings of the Lord along the mirrors of your heart, that you may know and that you may remember the goodness of the Lord your God. Daughter, too often you forget My former goodness. Write down a list of times when I have been good to you. Take record of My daily blessings, that you may remember who I am. I am faithful and just, and I let no man glory in My holiness. I am the Lord who loves you dearly. Let no circumstance cause you to forget that I am with you." (For scriptural reference, read Psalm 77:105, 1 Corinthians 1:29).

May I suggest that you also take record of the blessings of the Lord within your own life. This will be useful for your personal reference, both when things become easier, and also when they get tougher. In both circumstances, if we come out of sync with His Spirit and take our eyes off of Him, it becomes easy to lose focus and to forget the former goodness of the Lord our God. May we never forget His mercy. May we never forget His love.

SPREAD THE WORD

When we walk by the Spirit of God, on one side of the road there will be great stumbling blocks, deep ditches and stony, fiery traps. But in the other lane, there is abundant remuneration, multiple blessings and very great favour from the Lord. He never promised that this walk would be an easy one. He actually assured us that we will be persecuted for His name's sake (Matthew 10:22-42; 2 Timothy 3:12). But we are never alone, and God shows up time and time again for us to know that He is for us. He shows His merciful lovingkindness, He displays His mighty hand, so that even the eyes of the world know that He is God. When the Lord shows His works in your life, tell others what He has done! Testify, that they too may believe. The Bible says that we overcome the devil by the blood of the Lamb, and by the word of our testimony (Revelation 12:11). You just may help someone to overcome their trials when you testify of the goodness of our God.

The testimony of a child of God brings hope and feeds the fire of belief in the spirit of the hearer. Our faith arises as we are encouraged to believe that what God has done for the testifier, surely He can do it for us. Why narrow your scope of the possibilities of an infinite God? As He is boundless and matchless, grand above the heavens and the universe at large, can He not do the impossible? Can He who created the ear, not give hearing to the deaf? Can He who created the eye not give sight to the blind? Can he who created the body, not restore it to its full function? With man, these things are impossible, but with God, all things are possible (Matthew 19:26). Had not Matthew, Mark, Luke and John testified of all they had seen and heard of Jesus Christ, where would our faith in Him be today? From the book of Genesis to Deuteronomy, Joshua to Nehemiah, Esther and Job, the Psalms and the Books of Wisdom, the Prophets, the Gospels, the Acts and the Letters to the Saints - all biblical books testify of Jesus Christ. He is the living Word in whom our faith is daily renewed. Tell others of what He has done for you. No testimony is too small or insignificant. If the Lord has healed your big toe, tell someone. You never know if they may also be trusting the Lord for healing in theirs. If the Lord has helped you through an examination, delivered you from an addiction, supernaturally provided for you, protected you from danger or healed your toothache when you cried out to Him, then testify. You just do not know what other people may be going through, and that is not for you to determine. Our job is to share what God has done for us in the eyes and the ears of another. It is a seed of faith that is planted in the soul of a man, which by the Spirit of God, germinates, breaks the surface of doubt and despair, grows larger and stronger, and brings forth fruit that they too may share. It is God who gives the increase.

The enemy brings lies through false witnesses. They challenge the things of God, and attempt to explain Him away through science or man-made theology and philosophies (Colossians 2:8). Do not let this discourage you from letting others know the truth. Our testimony of Jesus Christ brings the truth, and makes way for others to encounter Him as well (Revelation 19:10). Let others know who He is and what He has done. Living the lifestyle of worship requires that we spread the word about the free gift of salvation, and the open invitation that God has given to everyone for eternal life.

We must therefore seek to obey our Lord Jesus' final instruction – to testify of Him to the far corners of the earth (Acts 1:8). Let us take up this mission of spreading the word of hope. Let us testify of the goodness of our Lord Jesus Christ, and not forget all that He has done for us. Let us seek to glorify Him with grateful hearts, in humility and obedience. Let us always remember that He loves us, and that throughout all of eternity, He alone is God.

Final Words

What a journey this has been. It has been an absolute honour and a great blessing to be able to share with you what the Lord Jesus Christ has taught to me. He has taught me the true meaning of worship – a life of commitment, discipline, humility, sacrifice, holiness and obedience to God. A life of fulfilment, satisfaction and great spiritual reward. A life of peace that is saturated with the grace and the love of the Father. A life of warfare and victory by the working of His Spirit on our behalf. It is a life that prepares us to walk with Him in His Kingdom while we are yet on this earth. One which brings glory to His name. It is the life that we were created to live. Yet, we have found ourselves oblivious to its richness by our assimilation into the systems of this world. We were born into the darkness of sin, never to remain, but to be translated into the abundant light and righteousness of our God. May we through all things, and at all times, seek to live the life that pleases God. May we seek to live the lifestyle of worship.

About the Author

Leah Lewis is a disciple of Jesus Christ and an end-time worshipper. She was born in the Republic of Trinidad and Tobago, where she began her worship ministry. She is also a public health professional, an entrepreneur and a musician. Hers is the voice behind the Holy Spirit-filled musical album: *"YHVH – Let All Nations Hear the Voice of the Lord God of Israel: I AM"*. It is a novelty album birthed in the secret place, filled with messianic worship songs, where each one is sung only by the gift of tongues. Leah shares the principles of worship in the spirit with the Body of Christ.

To contact the author, please visit her website:
www.leahwords.ml.

You can also send an email to:
info@leahwords.ml

Connect with Leah on Twitter, @leahwords.

Please feel free to share your testimony of how this book has helped you. May God bless you richly.

YOU'VE READ WHAT THE SPIRIT OF THE LORD HAS SAID. NOW IT'S TIME FOR YOU TO

Experience it!

THIS MUSICAL GEM IS THE FIRST OF ITS KIND. AN ALBUM BY WORSHIP SINGER LEAH LEWIS, CARRYING AN IMPORTANT PROPHETIC MESSAGE BY THE SPIRIT OF GOD: **"DO NOT FORGET ME"**. SURELY GOD IS SPEAKING. LET ALL NATIONS HEAR HIS VOICE.

THIS ALBUM IS HEAVILY ANOINTED AND WILL SURELY BRING HEALING TO YOUR SOUL. ITS MUSIC IS MIDDLE EASTERN AND ITS LANGUAGES CONTAIN TRACES OF MIDDLE EASTERN DIALECTS, ALL BY THE GIFT OF DIVERSE TONGUES (1 CORINTHIANS 12:7-11). ITS POETIC INTERPRETATIONS WILL BLESS YOU GREATLY.

AVAILABLE

 AT

WWW.MALKUT-PUBLISHING.COM

WORSHIP WILL NEVER BE THE SAME AGAIN. **GET YOUR COPY OF THE ALBUM THAT IS ABOUT TO SHAKE THE LIMITS OFF OF WORSHIP FOREVER.** BE A PART OF THE NEXT GREAT MOVE OF GOD, FOR SURELY "WITH STAMMERING LIPS AND ANOTHER TONGUE HE WILL SPEAK TO THIS PEOPLE" — ISAIAH 28:11.

www.ingramcontent.com/pod-product-compliance
Lightning Source LLC
Chambersburg PA
CBHW071455040426
42444CB00008B/1344